AW WITH WORDS

Young Writers' 16th Annual Poetry Competition

It is feeling and force of imagination that make us eloquent.

How can I not dream while writing? The blank page gives a right to dream.

Young**Writers**

South East England
Edited by Donna Samworth

YoungWriters

First published in Great Britain in 2007 by:
Young Writers
Remus House
Coltsfoot Drive
Peterborough
PE2 9JX
Telephone: 01733 890066
Website: www.youngwriters.co.uk

All Rights Reserved

© Copyright Contributors 2007

SB ISBN 978-1 84431 180 4

Foreword

This year, the Young Writers' *Away With Words* competition proudly presents a showcase of the best poetic talent selected from thousands of up-and-coming writers nationwide.

Young Writers was established in 1991 to promote the reading and writing of poetry within schools and to the young of today. Our books nurture and inspire confidence in the ability of young writers and provide a snapshot of poems written in schools and at home by budding poets of the future.

The thought, effort, imagination and hard work put into each poem impressed us all and the task of selecting poems was a difficult but nevertheless enjoyable experience.

We hope you are as pleased as we are with the final selection and that you and your family continue to be entertained with *Away With Words South East England* for many years to come.

Contents

Toyah Ballam (13)	1
Lindsay Wright (14)	2

Bartholomew School, Witney

Abigail Buckle (11)	4
Beatrice Grist-Perkins (11)	5
Holly Gorne (13)	6
Gerda Bachrati (12)	8
Alexandra Cherry (12)	10
Emily Walsh (12)	11

Brighton Hove & Sussex Sixth Form College, Hove

Lucie Glasheen (18)	12
Caitlin Hayward-Tapp (16)	13
Esther Coombs (16)	14
Lucy McClean (16)	15

Didcot Girls' School, Didcot

Hannah Barr (15)	16
Emma Gregory (15)	17

Helenswood Upper School, Hastings

Sarah Dean (16)	18
Jodie Winter (15)	20
Kimberley Stafford (16)	21
Leanne Cannon (14)	22
Frances Dynes (15)	23
Danielle Rounds (15)	24
Joanna Bowes (15)	25
Lisa Nutbrown (16)	26

Lake Middle School, Sandown

Alice Rivers (12)	27
George Flynn (13)	28
Charlotte Kent (12)	29
Melissa Calvert (13)	30
Ashley James (13)	31

Lucy Deakin (12)	32
Laura Swan (12)	33
Ben Hooper (13)	34
Ben Armstrong (13)	35
Jake Wade (13)	36
Ryan Oatley (12)	37
Rhiannan Matthews (13)	38
Nicola McDonald	39
Daniella Gilbey (11)	40
Ben Sewell (11)	41
Amber Pierce (11)	42
Kerry Johnson (12)	43
Julion Jayerajah, Ben Buckingham & Seb Rayner (12)	44
Nicholas Blyth (12)	45
Ella Hayward (12)	46
Kim Lacey (12)	47
Alasdair Malcolm (11)	48
Shannen Ward (12)	49
Maggie Read (12)	50
James Wall (12)	51
Reece Finnis (11)	52
Kane Goodyear (12)	53
Ellie Brown (12)	54
Jack McHugh (11)	55
Jacqueline Back (11)	56
Jenna Wood (12)	57
Nikki Williams (12)	58
Jake Pond (11)	59
Shophia Moule (11)	60
Aaron Mills (12)	61
Harry Manley (11)	62
Ellie Fielder (12)	63
Lucy Burke (11)	64
Thomas Battram (12)	65
Michael Barlow (12)	66
Anna-Louise Lee (13)	67

Lord Williams's School, Thame

Sophie Bignell (13)	68
Ellie Tiplady (13)	69
Amy Gascoyne (12)	70

Helena Mann (13)	71
Helena Schwarz (12)	72
Ellen Feuchtwanger (12)	73
Rhiannon Peters (11)	74
Laura Batt (12)	75

Northern House School (BESD), Oxford
Dayle Hall (12)	76
Jamie McLaughlan (11)	77
Mitchel Why (12)	78

Penn School, Penn
Alysia Bradbrook-Armit (14)	79
Michael Kane (14)	80
Ravneet Janda (15)	81
Lisa Ward (15)	82
James Pervoe (15)	83

Rye Saint Antony School, Headington
Nwadiogo Quartey-Ngwube (18)	84

St Leonards-Mayfield School, Mayfield
Katharine Eakin (12)	85
Olivia Mills (12)	86
Olivia Cottrell (12)	87
Elinor Bushell (11)	88

St Mary's Hall School, Brighton
Vicci Cowlett (13)	88

The Buckingham Secondary School, Buckingham
Sam Jordan (13)	90
Siân Mason (12)	91
Bryony Foote (12)	92
Olivia Venables (11)	93
Daniel Mills (11)	94
Archie Keir (12)	95
Becky Fowler (13)	96
Jodie Taylor (12)	97

Leah Robinson (13)	98
Leanne Mayhew (12)	99
Hannah Brinn (13)	100
Stacey-Leigh Dalton (12)	101
Harriet Mitchell (13)	102
Megan Bainbridge (13)	103
Polly Mullins (12)	104
Ryan Critoph (13)	105
Josie Swindell (12)	106
Jasmin Stevens (11)	107
Katrina Lambert (13)	108
Ellen Whitbread (12)	109
Nicola George (12)	110
Anna Cresswell (12)	111
Olie Newton (12)	112
Eunice Ngala (11)	113
Abby Ramanauckis (12)	114
Ben Ogle (12)	115
Hattie Jeffs (11)	116
Rhiannon Taylor (11)	117
D'Maria Fernander (11)	118
Ashleigh-Rose Turner (13)	119
Andrew Brooker (12)	120
Joe Townsend (12)	121
Alex Price (12)	122
Jack Reynolds (13)	123
George Chisholme (12)	124
Emma Curley (12)	125
Jennifer Mepham (13)	126
Aisha Thornton (12)	127
Samantha Holder (13)	128
Kimberley Price (13)	129
Joanne Higgins (13)	130
Zach Campbell (13)	131
Ben Baker (13)	132
Kirsty Barson (13)	133
Sophie Carr (12)	134
Gemma Chittenden (13)	135
William Edmondson (12)	136
Luke Hancock (12)	137
Leanne Day (13)	138
Andrew Kebbell (12)	139

Ben Oliver (12)	140
Matthew Shackell (12)	141
Ben Phillips (12)	142
Benjamin Rowell (13)	143
Kayleigh Honor (13)	144
Tom Reading (13)	145
Tate Butler (13)	146
Jack Carpenter (13)	147
Jonathon Clark (12)	148
Dean Faulkner (13)	149
Abbie Livingstone (11)	150
Hannah Biltcliffe (11)	151
Josh Hill (11)	152
Sebastian Holuj (12)	153
Rebecca Eggleton (11)	154
Kar Yeun Tang (12)	155
Billy Jones (12)	156
Dominic Dunn (12)	157
Rebecca Blackmore (12)	158
Jade Heritage (11)	159
Marcus Prodanovic (12)	160
Ben Oxley (12)	161
Katie Harland (11)	162
Megan Thompson (12)	163
Beth Cox (11)	164
Lee Morrison (12)	165
Kirsty Grant (12)	166
Kayley Roberts (12)	167
Paige Costello (12)	168
Evan Wootton-Haley (11)	169
Robert Lukey (11)	170
Sam Reddrop (12)	171
Hayley Siklodi (12)	172
Abigail Young (12)	173
Stephanie Robertson (11)	174
Geethapriya Thiruvalluvan (11)	175
Charlotte Birks (12)	176
Kyle Carter (12)	177
Cherry Eales (13)	178
Jasmine Harding (12)	179
Dale Armitage (11)	180
Wayde Cutler (11)	181

Amy Tickett (11)	182
Alex Clinkard (11)	183
Jordan Klette (11)	184
Christina Jones (11)	185
Natasha Hedge (11)	186
Daniel Rolston (13)	187
Greg King (13)	188
James Blundell (12)	189
Zoe McPartlane (13)	190
Conor Yull (13)	191
Jack Carroll-Taylor (12)	192
Jordan Stephens (12)	193
Jade Muckleston (12)	194
Kelly Allen (13)	195
Sharn Duggan (13)	196
Josh Whitehead (13)	197
Stevie Watts (13)	198
Kelly-Ann Morris (13)	199
Maddie Smith (13)	200
Stephanie Lambourne (13)	201
Samantha Horsler (13)	202
Sean Elmes (13)	203
Becky Davies (12)	204

The Warriner School, Banbury

Sophie Ellis (13)	205
Cara Davis (12)	206
Sian Murphy (13)	207
James Richardson (12)	208
George Kay (12)	209
Megan Collison (13)	210

The Poems

A Christmas In The Future

In the year of 2050
There is going to be the snowiest Christmas ever.
Global warming is going
To be a pain in the backside.
Wherever you will look
There will be ice and snow.
You will learn to get used to it
Waking up to snow every morning
And going to bed in the evening
With snow wherever you go.

Around Christmas
The snow will get thicker and thicker
And the ice will get icier and icier.
Children will be out covered from head to toe
Scarves, hats, gloves, wellies, big warm coats.
Making snowmen,
Hoping that the snowmen will come to life.

On Christmas Eve the skies will open
Out will come the biggest snowflakes that anyone has seen.
The jingle of bells
Tell the snowmen that the man,
The man who wears
The red and white fluffy coat is on his way.
The snowmen
Come to life, dancing around in the snow.

When I was a child
I wished for a white Christmas.
But now, because of global warming
We will always have white Christmases.
We will have white springs, white summers, white autumns
                                        and white winters.

Toyah Ballam (13)

What Is A Poem?

A poem
Is a poem
Written by a poet
To say something
It can be a long poem with lots of verses and lines and words and
rhymes and ideas
From your mind
Or it can be
Short
And . . .
Each line
Can rhyme
All the time
Or not at all
Also . . .
Poems can be simple
Written about one idea
Or they can be complicated
Hard to read and hear
A
    Poem
        Can
            Be
        Shaped
    Or
In a straight line.
A poem can be tall and thin
Or small and slim
But . . .
A poem can be accurately perfectly grammatically correct
Or mest up against rools
A poem is always a poem
Even if it's just some lines
One line is a sentence
But two's a poem just fine
A poem is never wrong
It's never ever bad
It's what you've written down

Whether you're happy or sad
A poem is what you want it to be
The rules will never change
Your poem is unique to you
Because two are never the same
Your poem is your right to say
Whatever is on your mind
A poem is your free speech
And this poem is mine.

Lindsay Wright (14)

Someone Else's Eyes

Look at the world through another's eyes
Walk the footsteps of a stranger
Will you see truth, will you see lies?

If you look at the world from the sky
Will you see peace or destruction
If you look at the world from a bird's eye?

If you look at the world from down low,
Will you see the dark dirt or sky
Through a snake's eye, slithering slow?

If you look at the world in a war
Will you see darkness or hope
Through the eye of a soldier, cold and poor?

So pause and look at everyone
And look at the world through their eyes
Is it filled with dread, laughter or fun?

Abigail Buckle (11)
Bartholomew School, Witney

The Meaning Of Life

What's the meaning of life?
Is it to live and die?
To see, to speak, to smell?
Is it for memories?
Just for good and bad memories,
Who knows.

What's the meaning of life?
Is it to learn, to feel, to experiment?
No one knows.

But if this is life, what is death?
Is it black, white or even purple?
Is there another life beyond the grave?
No one can speak of this land,
Or can they?

What's the meaning of life?
Is it to live and die?
To see, to speak, to smell?
Is it for memories?
Just for good and bad memories,
No one knows.

Beatrice Grist-Perkins (11)
Bartholomew School, Witney

The Ghost Girl

She was our friend,
A ray of sun,
Like a diamond
Strong and fun.

She was happy
Full of light,
A candle burning
Through the night.

Then it happened
Hard and quick,
We thought she
Could handle it.

Her pain grew,
Her eyes lost shine,
No more diamonds
In the mine.

Her tears grew thicker,
Faster too,
Her eyes cried oceans,
Sad and blue.

The laughter's gone,
It can't return,
Her tears put out
The candle's burn.

Her mournful cries,
Her beating heart,
Gently echo
Through the dark.

She wanders now
Across lost lands,
Searching for
Room to expand.

She'll spread her wings,
She'll fly away,
Her smile will come
Again one day.

But not quite yet
For she's still here,
Whispering softly
In your ear.

'I am the ghost girl
Set me free,
There is a place
Where I can be.

Birds will fly there,
Bells will ring,
Let me go
And I shall sing.

Peace and love
And praises be
To you kind soul
You rescued me.'

She was our friend,
But is no longer,
Ghost girl wishes
She were stronger.

Holly Gorne (13)
Bartholomew School, Witney

A Voice To Someone Who Hasn't Any

If I had a voice,
Instead of silence,
I'd do my bit
For my precious Earth.

Hidden away,
But alas, not invisible,
I, as any other, have suffered,
Of this prejudice and pride.

Stop the hatred,
The neglect.
Stop it,
Before it's too late!

Ignore normal, precious souls,
March by, noses up,
I am here,
You just can't, don't want to see.

Striding down the bustling street,
Looking around.
So many different people.
Feelings seeping out.

But no one caring,
No feeling,
No one understands,
The pain they're experiencing.

We're here,
Yes, here,
Hello,
We're here beside you,
Behind you,
You know we're here,
You just don't want to.

People bustling
But no one noticing,
Hundreds,
Thousands.
But still, so much pain,
We're strange,
But nothing new.
Just 'cause we're different.

Gerda Bachrati (12)
Bartholomew School, Witney

Winter

Winter is a white blanket laid across the Earth.
Snowballs launching, a grenade!
A child's Heaven!

Frozen lagoons of frost
Tears of God, an icy lake
A snowman's home
A flooded land of ice

Slowly dying as the horizon appears
Frost whispers in the sky
A soft snowing layer suffocating the land
Water, dead calm as can be.

Alexandra Cherry (12)
Bartholomew School, Witney

Cloud

I see the world,
Death
Destruction
Hate
The sky, my home, the wind, my bed.
I see the world,
Hope
Tears
Love
Body ever changing, never breathing a breath
I see the world,
Fire
Water
Sea
Drifting
No one thinks
No one dreams
No one thinks of me.

Emily Walsh (12)
Bartholomew School, Witney

Early Onset

Fshuck, fshuck, fshuck,
I grasp the paper cup.
Fshuck, fshuck, fshuck,
Both hands. Both hands get burnt.
It spills, it slurps, it scalds,
Fshuck, fshuck, fshuck,
My shaking paper cup.

Shfit, shfit, shfit,
For God's sake get a grip.
Shfit, shfit, shfit,
My beating, biting, fighting
Heart. It stops, it starts.
Shfit, shfit, shfit,
My shaking quaking fit.

The canteen line of endless eyes.
The end. The start.
My badge. My cart.
My nameless, blameless, shameless
Tart.
My endless line
Of canteen eyes.

Expletive omitted.
The start.
The end.
Replay this story
Again,
Again,
Again . . .

Lucie Glasheen (18)
Brighton Hove & Sussex Sixth Form College, Hove

Two Lovers

I saw two lovers, hand in hand,
Walk along the endless sand.
He thinks their love is endless too
Look at her eyes - it is not true.
For though they walk on hand in hand
Along the never-ending sand,
They look into each other's eyes
She whispers softly, 'Love tells lies.'

Two lovers on a different beach
Walk side by side, they do not speak.
Their hands hang limp, they do not touch,
They love each other very much.
Then one, becoming stronger, bold,
Takes the other's hand to hold.
People stop, they stand and stare
At this most fascinating pair.
The two who had shown no affection,
Two women bordering perfection,
The lovers smile - they understand.
Their love is like the endless sand.

Caitlin Hayward-Tapp (16)
Brighton Hove & Sussex Sixth Form College, Hove

Affairs Of The Hands

Aching, she waits,
Quivering hands,
He moves slowly,
Seconds tick by.
Unbearable.

The bells pealing!
His tall form looms,
Their gazes lock.
Fate's cogs release -
Separation.

Her grieving pleas;
Begs him to stay.
Duty demands,
Pulls them apart.
Agonizing.

Threat stalks past her.
Slim. Seductive.
Alarm bells ring,
His betrayal . . . ?
Paranoia.

Such sad sorrow.
Those two as one?
She's forgotten.
Pain and rage rise –
Desolation.

Pendulum swings.
All clock hands tick,
Life swings, life ticks,
She waits, time slips . . .
Tick-tock, tick-tock.

Esther Coombs (16)
Brighton Hove & Sussex Sixth Form College, Hove

Other Mother

I am the proud owner of two mothers,
Mother and the other mother.
Mother sleeps whilst Daddy cooks,
My other mother is in the other room,
We are not allowed in there,
That's my other mother's secret lair.
But when my other mother comes out,
I jump and scream and run about,
I love my other mother.

Sometimes people stay and play,
Like my other mother's other sister,
And my other mother's little brother.
I hang onto her top and don't let go.
I tell her all my great achievements,
All my thoughts and life ambitions.
She smiles and nods.
I, am the proud owner of a mother,
And another, mother.

Lucy McClean (16)
Brighton Hove & Sussex Sixth Form College, Hove

Miss Havisham's Lament

Mice run around in lead boots,
Spiders scurry in stampede formation.
Whilst I just sit,
Alone.
Too weak to brush the time from the mirror,
Too old to light the dying oil lamp.
So I just sit,
Remembering . . .
Estella rears her head round the door, her eyes smug,
Brimming with glee -
She never had my beauty.
Yet life has seemed to kill me,
My skin and my dress have swapped colours,
Stained and aged, blemished and rotting
I just sit.
But not alone for long.
Although my wedding feast decays and rots
My mind remains as sharp as ever.

Running my tongue over my cracked lips I can taste him
B*****d.
Ruining my life, jilting me, *me!*
Leaving me here, in time's own prison.
But I'll seek my revenge . . .

A boy from the village is coming to tea,
To play.
And I'll just sit, watch, study, decipher his every move,
Miss Havisham won't die alone.

Hannah Barr (15)
Didcot Girls' School, Didcot

Empire Of The Forest

Whistles of a lifetime
Whispers in the leaves
Haunting moans and aching groans
Warning feathered thieves

Many stand together
Yet none can ever talk
Lonely days and lonely nights
Lonely time for thought

Wrinkled skin of wisdom
Bare flesh showing age
Roots that reach through earthy bars
To free them from their cage

Deep and almost silent
Their only voice would be
But never said and spoken not
Desirous to be free

Angels touch their branches
And leave them blossomed hair
Luscious fruit left gleaming bright
Upon the summer fair

Yet when the sky turns cloudy
And sorrow settles in
The lonely voice and bitter eyes
Remember summer's kin

Whistles of a lifetime
Whispers in the leaves
Haunting moans and aching groans
Warning feathered thieves.

Emma Gregory (15)
Didcot Girls' School, Didcot

The Depth Of The Blade

The scratches turn into cuts,
The cuts into wounds,
The wounds into perfectly formed scars
And then they will fade like everything else,
The passion,
The desire,
The want,
The love,
This torture that goes through my veins,
The pain inside that does not surface,
The emptiness that I now feel,
The freedom that I long for,
Will you let me go if I want
Or will you make me stay?
Stay in this world of suppression,
Of anger and hate,
Of deceit and lies,
Of pain and corruption,
Or will you let me be free?
Free to be happy again,
To hurt no more,
To take the blade from my heart,
And place it back in your hand.
Only to be placed there once again,
When you feel the time is right,
To bring the fear back in my bones,
To place me under your control,
To scare me once again.
I am under your control,
Just like I always was,
I wait here to be set free,
Or to be condemned.

Just like before the fear is rising,
The tears are forming in my eyes,
Every word is a dagger in my heart,
That you no longer see,
That you no longer feel.
The depth of the blade is deeper then it appears,
It is not pulled out so easily,
It will stay there from now till then . . .

Sarah Dean (16)
Helenswood Upper School, Hastings

September Day

A mother cries,
A child dies.
An hour ago, maybe more,
Al-Queda decided to settle a score.
Air Force One is in full flight,
America will start a fight.
The world was shocked and bombed away,
Because of that fateful September day.

The UN tried to stop the war,
America said, 'Iraq's got to know no more.'
Britain joined America's fight,
The world was treated to the sight,
Of guns and bloodshed, wrong and right.
When the planes blew up the air,
The world was broken but the world did care.
The world was shocked and bombed away
Because of the fateful September day.

Jodie Winter (15)
Helenswood Upper School, Hastings

Break Free

My life is chained in this pantomime,
The heavens buy their tickets for each day.
I hide behind this costume, this make-up,
Watching as my life ticks away.
Some get frozen still with their stage fright,
Others take it all in their stride,
I'm going round in circles; don't know which way to turn,
When you're born you sign up for this endless ride.

But I know my life's not written in the words on this page,
It cannot be a plan for the spotlight on this stage,
Everything they teach you, everyone you think you know,
You're a puppet on a string; they're just the script to your show.

I drag myself for my curtain call,
I play a role for Heaven here in Hell,
The cameras flash and the smoke goes up,
I'm tired of living in this fairytale,
I want to get out, live life all my way,
But how to know now what's real and what's true?
The Grim Reaper's your director when your part's not in the play,
You've played your part; it's time to start anew.

Every day I sit behind these bars I'm losing my mind,
By moonlight I am leaving all this madness behind.
Everything they teach you, everyone you think you know,
Your past don't mean a thing, it's just the script to your show.

So take off the mask, turn off the lights,
Fire the cast and stop living a lie,
Bring the curtains down, no more running away,
Face your fears and live for the day,
It's time to close the page and break free from this stage.

Kimberley Stafford (16)
Helenswood Upper School, Hastings

Friendship

No matter who you are,
No matter what you do,
True friends will be there
And stick by you.

The truth is clear
And simple.

The idea is predicable,
A smile that you make
On someone else's face,
Is worth more than a wish come true.

It will be hard,
But we'll get through
Tough times will come,
And hopefully go,
And after that
Truly our friendship will grow.

I offer a vow
That will last forever.
Nothing will get between us,
Or stand in our way,
We will live on.
But if we grow apart,
Remember just this –
You will always be in my heart.

Leanne Cannon (14)
Helenswood Upper School, Hastings

The Life Of A Cat

Wake up with a long yawn
Stretch twisted body parts
Last night's dream gone, but don't mourn
Today is a new start.
Pitter-patter round for new smells
Outside the sun shines brightly
Bunnies frolic like young gazelles
Suddenly attacked and held tightly
Squirm when kissed on the nose
Jump from their arms
Sneaking under their toes like unlucky charms
Snuggle back down on the mat
This is the life, the life of a cat.

Frances Dynes (15)
Helenswood Upper School, Hastings

When I Am Dead

Who knows what goes on
After we're dead,
Do we lie in the ground
No thoughts in our head?
Do our souls leave our bodies
And go into the sky
Flying with angels
Way up so high?
Is there a Heaven, is there a Hell?
Is the Garden of Paradise
The place where we'll dwell?
Will we roam the Earth
As lonely ghosts?
Will we reunite with the people
We've missed the most?
Do we return as another
Forgetting our past?
An animal or plant,
The possibilities are vast!
I think all these thoughts
As I lay in my bed,
What's going to happen
When I am dead?

Danielle Rounds (15)
Helenswood Upper School, Hastings

Standing Tall

Where does sadness come from
The heart or the mind?
When you look in the mirror
What do you expect to find?
Someone with a broken heart
Or someone with a fear
Or even both for all I know
But I always tend to hear,
That someone is upset
About the truth or even love,
And there we are all wondering
If there's someone up above.
Watching everything we do
And everything we say,
Waiting for us to hear their advice,
That there is another way.
That we don't have to live in sadness,
We should accept a helping hand.
We can learn from our mistakes
Until we understand.
That this life has been handed to us,
We should live it to the full,
But not by hiding from our fears
By smiling proudly and standing tall.

Joanna Bowes (15)
Helenswood Upper School, Hastings

For My Dad

I still remember the day I was told,
My hero was no longer here for me to hold.
Wearing your favourite blue top too
I realised this is all I had left of you.

I always felt safe with you around,
Suddenly insecurity was found.
I knew I had all the family
But me without you felt lonely.

My love for you is very strong,
Your not being here just feels wrong.
The strongest man taken away,
I still cry and get upset to this very day.

I hope you're sitting on your cloud,
Looking down and feeling proud
Of what us kids can all achieve,
It's because you taught us to believe.

One last hug is all I need,
I did this poem for you to read.
I'll hold on tight, it won't be long
Until we're together, with our special bond.

I'll look up to the sky,
I'll hold my head up high,
I'll try my hardest not to cry
If only I could have said goodbye.

All my love forever,
Lisa.

Lisa Nutbrown (16)
Helenswood Upper School, Hastings

Essential Foundation

Life
Before you can begin to envisage your future you must build.
Build the essential foundation, strengthen your start,
Standing at the bottom however much fate has pulled
You cannot see the end of life's structure,
The centre is too broad,
In the centre is too much work to be done,
To look further and be ignored.
Take time,
Pick your route,
Choose your material with care.
Think.
Everything you must protect
Build a skyscraper, don't make a shack.

Alice Rivers (12)
Lake Middle School, Sandown

The Labour Of Life

I am a boy
Trapped helplessly in a society where money is rare
I search for hours on end trying to find scraps
Like a bird hunting its prey
Yet there is no prey for me
No nothing
No food
No water
No clean clothes
All this I try to manage on my own
As you see my parents passed away last year
Now it is just me still grieving the loss of my parents
Doing responsibilities that they would have done
At this present time I am twelve years old
And already acting as a adult
It's just me and my brother who is five
I live his life
He is all I have left
I am all he has left
I am a father figure to him
If I die like my parents who will look after him now?
I live every day like it's my last
Hoping someone out there will help.

George Flynn (13)
Lake Middle School, Sandown

We're Not All Bad

All of the people around the world think
We are not all bad, only some.
I'm thinking about the youth of today
One or two are bad
But think everyone, we need your praise
Not a bad influence, everybody help us
We don't want a bad reputation
So you over there, yes you, we're not all bad!
Don't forget, we're not all bad!

Charlotte Kent (12)
Lake Middle School, Sandown

Why?

Why are we here?
What is the point?
We love and we get hurt.
We don't love and we're lonely.
We make friends and we lose friends.
We love, we hate.
But why?
We're born, but then we die.
We make mistakes and we regret.
We create and we destroy.
We start young, we get old.
But why?
Why do all these things happen?
Are we all part of God's plan, who is God?
There are endless questions but none we'll ever find the answer too.
What is the point?
What are we supped to do here?
I guess we'll never know.

Melissa Calvert (13)
Lake Middle School, Sandown

The Tigers

Where is everyone
They've got shot by a gun
Bang!
They're gone
I'm all alone
No one besides me
Shivering in the cold
Wishing there was someone
They're gone
Crying all night long
Only the trees in sight
They're gone
Bang!
I'm gone.

Ashley James (13)
Lake Middle School, Sandown

One Person Can Make A Difference

I stand here and you place your hand in mine, there's a connection,
I can tell.
And then if somebody else stands here and puts their hand in yours,
the connection strengthens.
I can tell that if somebody else, a stranger, walks past and sees us
Then they will put their hand into ours and the connection lengthens.
It will keep going, the chain of hands in hand around the world,
peacefulness and silence.
The chain will always be there, love passing through the linked fingers,
right round the world
Like a circuit of the greatest power possible.
Thoughts flood through everyone's mind, a wondering,
confused feeling,
We think more deeply than ever before why we are here.
We think more deeply than ever before about each other.
We think more deeply then ever before.
A hand relaxes somewhere in the chain and that person drops out,
The love and power can no longer flow, carefree through the world
and then it starts,
The wars, evil and malevolence.
The arguments start, the violence and the misunderstandings,
the hatred and deception.
It starts because one person left the chain and angered the rest,
One person can make such a difference to a world,
I started the love chain but you finished it.

Lucy Deakin (12)
Lake Middle School, Sandown

Third World Poverty

Filthy and cold,
Starved and neglected,
Not in our world
But in a poor third.

Deaths every day,
No food in sight,
Walking for miles,
Searching for the light.

Still they love, they care
And they respect each other.
With food or without,
We are the same as one another.

Pretend to be there
Does it feel like it's you?
Do you now care
Because you know how it feels?

Next time you're unhappy,
Angry or upset,
Think about them
And be thankful for what you get!

Laura Swan (12)
Lake Middle School, Sandown

Walking Down A Street

Walking down a street . . .
I can hear the sound of rap music coming from the dark, dingy alley.
I can see the art of graffiti all along cracked, grotesque walls.
I can smell the fumes of drugs making me choke.
What has happened here?
What went wrong?

Ben Hooper (13)
Lake Middle School, Sandown

41st Superbowl MVP

Through the eyes and a day in the life of me
I became Superbowl MVP.
I led my team to twelve and four
Then I achieved a feat that my team hadn't done before!
On the biggest stage of them all
Showing my skills off to the world and leaving them all in awe.
I've been called the best player in the game.
Then in this event I gave this title no shame
I told the world that was my time
But undoubtedly I did shine
Now I'm a world champion and as before
Through the eyes and a day in the life of me
I became Superbowl MVP!

Ben Armstrong (13)
Lake Middle School, Sandown

Life Through The Eyes Of A Teen

Watching the news every day
Political giants trying to get their way,
Nothing good, just everything bad
The constant pain makes a guy sad.

The streets at day, the streets at night,
If you're alone you're bound to get into a fight,
Down every alley, dangerous thugs,
Your so called mates pressuring you into drugs.

Sometimes life is not worth living
The greedy citizens not into giving
How can they all sleep at night?
If they really knew they'd be in for a fright.

On every corner another bully
Laughing in your face because your jumper's woolly
In today's life if you're not hip-hop
The taunts and abuse will never stop.

Because of our age, people think we're the same
But it doesn't mean we have to take the blame,
Give us a chance and you might find
That most of us are really quite kind.

Jake Wade (13)
Lake Middle School, Sandown

The Youth Of Today

Why is it always our fault?
Why do we get the blame?
'Turn that awful music down'
'Stop kicking that ball!'
'Don't play that stupid game!'

Hanging round on street corners
Nothing we can find to do,
Not doing anybody any harm
We're not annoying you.

You look at us with frowning faces
Accusing us with your eyes
Expecting us to cause trouble
Insulting us with your lies.

It wasn't like this in our day,
Is what they always say
Children should be given a job to do
You work first then you can play.

Please don't judge us so quickly
You don't even know our names
You won't bother trying to speak to us
You just shoot us down in flames!

Why not stop and think a while?
Not all of us are the same.
Most of us are decent people,
Just trying to play life's game.

Ryan Oatley (12)
Lake Middle School, Sandown

Beat Bullying

She sits in the corner
Contemplating her life.
She sighs in deeply, tears in her eyes,
Like cold daggers,
That cut through the truth,
And hide all her lies.

Her face is white and gaunt,
Her hands are shaking,
The blade
Lay in her palm,
She knows that if she does,
It will stop the taunt.

If only she could fight the pain,
To be laughing, joking, happy again.
As the blade drops to the floor,
She stands strong not insecure, and crying no more.

Her face is no longer white and gaunt,
Her eyes gleaming green,
Sparkling and vibrant.

She stood up for what she believed in,
And now no one controls her life.
She stands in front of the mirror
Proud of who she is, and knows it'll be alright.
Don't be afraid to tell someone.

Rhiannan Matthews (13)
Lake Middle School, Sandown

My Tree Poem

One day I was sat here
Happy as can be,
Sat here all alone
Just being me.

Wasn't doing anything,
Swaying side to side,
Free as a fish
Not being criticized.

Then one little boy
Came over and shouted,
'Boys come over here'
Then four other boys came
Stopped and glared.

I'm scared; they stab and stab me,
I'm trembling like an old lady,
They tattoo my body with chunky pens,
They break my bones and run away,
They look back and glare with no care.

Nicola McDonald
Lake Middle School, Sandown

Me

If I could talk, I would shout,
People hold me all the time, I just want to get out.
When I want something I try to talk
But the only thing is I can't talk.

People are in my face
But I was enjoying myself in my own space.
When I cry, my mummy just ignores me
I get shouted at when I crawl around the house.

When I cry I want my bottle,
My mummy hurts me, I get really, really scared.

She swings,
She throws,
She slaps,
She shouts,
She's left me!

Daniella Gilbey (11)
Lake Middle School, Sandown

Sing

Can I sing?
I can sing.
Even though my tongue may ache,
Even though my voice might break.
What difference does it make?
I will sing.
Sing for the joy it will bring.
I may shout,
Shout it out.
Yet it may be quiet,
As a smile.
A smile that is genial,
And I can sing,
And I will sing,
I sing.

Ben Sewell (11)
Lake Middle School, Sandown

A Silent World

I'm in a room,
A quiet room,
Not because there's only a couple of people in the room.
No.
It's because, well, I can't speak.
They are all staring at me, like a bug, a maggot.
I try to wiggle my hands,
That's my language,
It seems to be my own private language.
Nobody understands me,
They all laugh at me.
There's no change there, everybody does that to me.
But why me, why me?
I know why, because,
. . . I'm different.

Amber Pierce (11)
Lake Middle School, Sandown

All I Want . . .

All I want is a friend,
Just someone to talk to.
All I want is a mate,
Just like all of you.
All I want is somebody
To comfort me when I'm down.
All I want is a pal
Whose house I can go round.
All I want is a buddy,
Nothing less or more.
All I want is a shoulder to cry on,
Is that too much to ask for?

Kerry Johnson (12)
Lake Middle School, Sandown

Poetry

I am sitting all alone and I can't feel any bones
I get ignored when I knock on the door.
I feel all cold when I get told
That I'm not wanted anymore.

Time flies and it's getting old
I want a friend, to connect with my soul,
I don't want to grow old.
I don't like to do this
But that's the way I feel.

Julion Jayerajah, Ben Buckingham & Seb Rayner (12)
Lake Middle School, Sandown

The Tramp

Sitting in the corner on a back street
No one will listen to my pleas,
I am ignored in this world and no one cares.
If only my voice could be heard,
If only I had a part in this world,
All because I'm a tramp!

Nicholas Blyth (12)
Lake Middle School, Sandown

Poem

I get bullied at school
I can't stand up for myself.
I wish that I could
But I have no voice.
No one treats me the same.
They don't understand me,
Just ignore me.
Because I have no voice.
I want to be normal
A girl that could talk.
But that will never happen
I'm the girl with no voice.

Ella Hayward (12)
Lake Middle School, Sandown

If Only I Could Turn Back Time

I sit here rocking the baby,
Mixed thoughts running through my head.
He's crying, crying out loud,
I try to get him to go to sleep but he won't, he keeps on crying.
If only I could turn back time.

I wish I had not let Charlie and Tommo go,
I should have gone to the big house and told that Colonel
                                             and Wolf Woman,
All I have left is Big Joe and Mother.
If only I could turn back time.

My baby may not have a proper family,
My baby may not have a father,
My baby may never see his uncle again.
If only I could turn back time.

I hope they are OK,
I hope they come back soon.

Kim Lacey (12)
Lake Middle School, Sandown

Trench Life

Rats, rats,
Bloody, cursed rats,
Speaking,
Smelling,
Spreading disease.
We try to catch them,
We try to slay them,
They are more of an enemy
Than the ruddy Hun.
The guns,
Silent,
Oppressive,
Condescending.
The stench,
Worse than a cow's barn.
The sight of all those,
Groaning,
Pleading,
Running,
Chattering,
Silent men.
The machine guns,
Gaping,
Pointing,
Opening,
Firing,
Destroying.
Our lives
Are not our own.
Our guns are
Loud,
Large
And shelling lead.
The icy claws
Of death,
Drawing,
Painting,
Carving our destiny.

Alasdair Malcolm (11)
Lake Middle School, Sandown

Here I Am

Here I am again
With no friends again.
All alone again,
I can't be heard again.

I'm longing for a friend,
Hoping more than longing.
Why can't I be heard?
I have a voice but everyone's ignoring.

I'm standing here alone,
Someone walks by me.
They look me in the eye,
They feel the pain I hide in me.

Shannen Ward (12)
Lake Middle School, Sandown

Can I Be Heard?

I walk through the playground
I do feel depressed,
I bet you can guess
What has happened to me.

Yes, I've been bullied,
You hurt me inside.
You'd wish you'd walked away
When you see the light on the other side.

But now I've been bullied
It never goes away,
It stays with you, by your side,
So tell someone now.

Maggie Read (12)
Lake Middle School, Sandown

Give Someone A Voice

Big Joe
I hug my knees and close my eyes
I wish my dog was here
She has gone from me, now I'm all alone
Seems all my life I'll live in fear.

I hug my knees and close my eyes
I am all alone up in the tower
He has gone from me now, my dog has gone
Time is passing hour by hour.

James Wall (12)
Lake Middle School, Sandown

A Homeless Dog

Help me please
I've lost my home.
My owners do not want me,
Now I am all alone.
My fur is torn like the grass,
My teeth are as yellow as the sun,
My tongue is cut from licking open cans,
My hair is as raggy as a sheep and I am so, so alone.

Reece Finnis (11)
Lake Middle School, Sandown

The Unhappy Turtle

I don't know why I am here,
I just can't get out.
I'm filled with fear.
The sun in my eyes
Fills my eyes up with tears.
I just want to go home.
Oh I am so very mad,
I once was happy
But now I am sad.
I just want to get out
I want to find Dad!

Kane Goodyear (12)
Lake Middle School, Sandown

Whale In The River Thames

I'm swimming along down a river but where?
All of the people watch me and stare.
I try to get their attention,
Ask them where I am but none of them can hear me.
I wish I could find my way home,
I wonder if I'll ever get out of this place.
I start to feel dizzy, I'm moving around
With the propellers above me, I can't hear a sound.
Suddenly I'm tangled in a net,
I'm pulled out of the water, out of the wet!
Oh no, I'm dying, I can't get a breath,
I shouldn't have come here,
I knew I'd face death!

Ellie Brown (12)
Lake Middle School, Sandown

Quiet Life

My mouth opens
No sound comes out,
I wish I could speak
I wish I could shout.
The others are fine
They can still talk,
I suppose I should be happy,
At least I can walk.
I have no friends
They don't care
I could just hit them
But I wouldn't dare!
It's so annoying
That I can't speak,
Now I can't tell them
If there's a leak.
I wish people cared
I really do,
But now you have read this
You should care too!

Jack McHugh (11)
Lake Middle School, Sandown

No Voice

I watch them play
I'll let them say,
'He has no voice.'

They'll call me names,
But nothing will change,
He has no voice.

I will not cry,
I'm not shy,
'Cause it's true,
I have no voice.

Jacqueline Back (11)
Lake Middle School, Sandown

The Ignored Cat

I'm sat here in the cold
No way to get in.
Everyone is happy
Warm in their house.
But not me.
I'm sat here in the cold
Trying to get in.
Making noises,
Pulling faces,
But.
They don't listen.

Jenna Wood (12)
Lake Middle School, Sandown

Homeless

Wondering around the streets
Nowhere to go, nowhere to be,
People come and people go,
No one stops to stroke me.
To pick me up and cuddle me,
They all give me funny looks
And tell their children to keep away.
No one wants to stroke a shaggy-looking flea-biting dog.
Drunks pass, hitting out at me,
Lashing at me with sticks and trying to shoot me with their little guns.
Is there no place for an unloved, no-voiced dog?

Nikki Williams (12)
Lake Middle School, Sandown

Speechless

I have no voice,
I have no words,
I have no friends,
I have no life!

I spend my days at home,
I spend my nights at home,
I rarely leave the house
And when I do, I get bombarded with insults!

They say I'm mute,
They say I'm tongue-tied,
They say . . . they say I'm *taciturn!*

I'm not!
If only they could see,
I was born to be like this!

Jake Pond (11)
Lake Middle School, Sandown

Why Me?

Why me?
Why does everyone stare, stare like I'm a statue?
But I'm not a statue, I'm a human!
It all went wrong after the accident,
My dad told me I hit my head then all my nerves went wrong.
That's why I'm not normal, all because I can't speak.
I try to make friends, but they all walk away.
It's not fair on me, because all that I can talk to is myself.
Why me?

Shophia Moule (11)
Lake Middle School, Sandown

Voices

I had an accident when I was five
My mum was thankful I was still alive
Could I get my voice back?
Anger is building up more and more
Not about my family, it's some bullies
Today I tried to tell but I couldn't
They didn't know what I was saying
The bullies beat me up again
And punched and kicked
Later on I told my mum
I knew she'd understand
That was why the bullies stopped
Because she held my hand.

Aaron Mills (12)
Lake Middle School, Sandown

My Friend

I have a friend called Tommy
He is now about fifteen years old,
He cannot speak but still I like him,
He is the only one who understands what I am going through.
Some kids bully him and some feel sad for him,
Every day I wonder why he decides not to speak,
He does not have an illness; in fact maybe he can speak,
He cannot speak but he sure can listen to everything I say
That's my friend Tommy.

Harry Manley (11)
Lake Middle School, Sandown

No Voice

They call me names
They push me round
I have no voice
So there's no sound.

I let them punch
I let them slap
'Cause I'm quite big
They all shout fat!

They tease and laugh
They'll just do as they please
It'll never stop
Though I'm down on my knees.

Ellie Fielder (12)
Lake Middle School, Sandown

Through The Eyes Of A Baby

Why am I being crowded? Am I royalty
And why are they talking alien?
Why does everyone always pick me up?
Because sometimes I want some peace
And why is no one listening to me?
I am hungry and I want some food
Do I have to start crying?
Because I really don't want to.
I see these people slowly creeping up on me
Slowly getting closer and closer
And soon they're blurred
Their faces as big as
Their breath warming my face
It smells of food
I am not foreign
Never stupid
Just a
Baby.

Lucy Burke (11)
Lake Middle School, Sandown

No Voice

I lay; I lay right there on the hay,
Watching, listening for feet on the move,
I have no emotion but I want to run away,
For there's a lot of pain which nothing can soothe.

Watch and listen is all I can do,
Can't walk, can't talk, I just stay,
Without this barn I would flee you
But I can't, I'm emotionless on the hay.

I'm whipped, I'm hit, everything's bad,
All of this happens to me and is still happening,
I can't be mean, I can be glad,
I can only get hurt.

Thomas Battram (12)
Lake Middle School, Sandown

Youth

Today we all have a rating
Young people now are always hated
Why is it just one or two?
I can understand some but just a few
That vandalise and hurt people
But there are others who are nice people
They are kind but are still rated
But as they are teenagers they must be hated.

Michael Barlow (12)
Lake Middle School, Sandown

Through Her Eyes

Every night she'd sit there and cry
Wondering why she couldn't just die.
Bullies to her left, bullies to her right.
She'd just stand there, not one to fight.

It's not her fault, she's not like the rest.
She just wanted to clean up all this mess.
The bullies wouldn't stop, they just carried on.
She hated that this went on for so long.

There was only one way to stop this and that was to go
But she would have to find a way that nobody would know.
So there she is, insecure, torn and brave
But she didn't stand up to the bullies,
She turned to the grave.

Anna-Louise Lee (13)
Lake Middle School, Sandown

Lost Words

A butterfly's shadow moves quickly or slowly or fast like lightning
but can never be heard
It glides through the air just like my mouth but cannot say a word.

Like the starry sky, my voice lost behind the clouds and never to return
It wants to come out, it wants to break free but instead out it burns.

Burning up through my throat so angry I want to be heard
But so scared like a gun is pointing at my head.
I want to escape just like a frightened bird.
I'm the person who cannot be heard
I'm the person who cannot speak
My future does not look very bright
And my mind is very bleak.

Sophie Bignell (13)
Lord Williams's School, Thame

Stars And Daffodils

A girl so small amidst a war,
Abandoned in a city that fears footsteps.
Her ringlets on her damp cheek,
Delicate lips, frozen,
Raincoat, wet.
Her beret covered in soot,
Her star alive with truth.

A girl so small amidst a war,
At six years old, she's seen a murder.
Her mother's bruised body,
Her eyes black,
Her fingers purple,
She doesn't know how to cry,
Her star alive with courage.

A girl so small amidst a war,
The fog is a murderous blanket.
She hears a voice,
She sees a man with hazel eyes,
She feels his truncheon on her body,
She tastes the rain.

A girl so small amidst a war,
A daffodil weeps on her grave
But her star is alive with faith.

Ellie Tiplady (13)
Lord Williams's School, Thame

Dead Or Alive I Wonder

Why is my family
Crying at me?
I'm right in front of them
I can't be dead you see.

Lucy's got an exam this year
She'll be alone,
Oh dear,
Oh dear.

Tom's got a football game
In a town called Thame
Oh what a shame,
It was his ticket to fame.

I'm in this box,
I can't undo the iron locks,
I'm in this four-sided devil
For now and ever.

I see a light, it's so bright,
That I've lost my sight,
I feel a comforting hand
It's taking me up the winding stairs.

Amy Gascoyne (12)
Lord Williams's School, Thame

What Is Here Is Not

Standing here in this field
With the grass up to my knees
I see it all, I see what happened
So many memories.

I see the school's main building
I see Miss McDowell
I see my best friend Jamie Edwards
And the dog that used to howl.

I see all of the children playing
I see the bully bullying my sister
I see the girl, the one I loved
Oh how much I've missed her.

I hear that sound, that dreadful sound
The sound of the planes overhead
The sirens screeching their terrible sound
The sound that calls for the dead.

Everyone is screaming
Running around in panic
I see myself under the table
I must have just got out in the nick
I hear it overhead

It's coming, it's coming . . .

It seems like a lifetime before it hit
It hit the school with a blast
That dreadful bomb that awful bomb
The bomb that brings last to last

And now I'm here on my own
With no school in my sight
They have all gone, they have all left me
They have all gone towards the light.

Helena Mann (13)
Lord Williams's School, Thame

I Wish

I wish I was in Africa
Like I was before
I wish I was in Ghana
All of that and more.

My memories are unforgettable
My scar on my head
That's rememberable
Thankfully I wasn't dead.

I wish I was back there
In the hot baking sun
Instead of right here
Eating a cold stale bun.

Helena Schwarz (12)
Lord Williams's School, Thame

Torture To Death

As I look up at that dark plank roof
My mind fills with hatred.
When I look at those white faces grinning down at me
My stomach turns inside out.

They have taken my freedom,
My liberty,
My life.

They drain all my spirit,
As terror grabs me I toss and turn, scream and shout,
But I can't get out.
The rusty chains and manacles draw me back to calm.

They have taken my freedom,
My liberty,
My life.

As the whip goes down one final time,
Cutting deeper, drawing blood.
Blood. The colour of roses, a sharp pain as their thorns dig deep.

They have taken my freedom,
My liberty,
My life.

I fear the whip, I cower back,
I hear their scornful laughing,
Despair wraps me in its grasp,
I feel helpless, an orphan, all alone.

They have taken my freedom,
My liberty,
My life.

Death surrounds me,
Calling my name.
I tunnel into darkness as I
Answer
Its call . . .

Ellen Feuchtwanger (12)
Lord Williams's School, Thame

In The Eyes Of A Hamster

I'm running in my hamster wheel
The same as every day,
In the day I'm tired and want to go to sleep
But the children always wake me up to make me go and play.

Something vicious has arrived,
Something that I hate,
She comes up and claws at my cage
Even when it's late.

At night I normally run around
Hyper as a bee,
But now that the cat is here
I'm smaller than can be.

In another week or two
They'll get tired and leave me on my own,
Then I'll probably never get fed
And die to live alone.

Rhiannon Peters (11)
Lord Williams's School, Thame

Being Bullied

I lie awake in my bed,
Filled with fear, hate and dread.

My alarm goes off, it's 7am,
Time to get up, get dressed and meet them.

When I get to school, they're standing in a crowd,
I try to dodge round them, I make not a sound.

But they notice I'm there and make silly remarks,
I try to ignore them, concentrating hard.

I say that I'm ill to get out of class,
But the teachers just joke and say I'm being daft.

I sit in my seat, staring to space,
They throw rubbers and sharpeners right at my face.

The day is over, not a minute too soon,
Time to go home and cry in my room.

I feel so alone with no one to tell,
I hate being bullied, it's the ultimate hell.

Laura Batt (12)
Lord Williams's School, Thame

Through The Eyes Of Gerrard

Changing clothes, putting on the kit
And having a team talk from the manager.
Excited, we've got to get out there and win.
Lining up in the tunnel, I'm leading out, talking to the little girl mascot
　　　　　　　　　　　　　　　　　　　　　　　　　　at my side.
Nervous we might lose, Chelsea are on form.
Speaking to John Terry, Chelsea England captain, confident Chelsea
　　　　　　　　　　　　　　　　　　　　　　　　　　will win.
Time to go onto the pitch, echoing down the tunnel, people shouting
　　　　　　　　　　　　　　　　　　　　　　and blowing their horns.
The mascot happily skips at my side onto the pitch,
We stand in a line singing the national anthem, a great big cheer
　　　　　　　　　　　　　　　　　　　　　　　　　　fills the stadium.
I shake hands with the linesman, referee and John Terry;
I hope he is a fair ref
I hope Crouchie is on the ball today.
It's about to begin, the ball is on the spot.

Dayle Hall (12)
Northern House School (BESD), Oxford

The Best Night Ever

We are late rushing through the doors
The noise hits us, the sound of a body banging down on the floor
                                          sounding like a drum
The crowd are screaming
The big bloke threw the small bloke from shoulder height
Flipping him over as he went
That was bad.

The next match
Everyone is excited the wrestlers walked in
The music was booming loud
Robbie Williams 'Let me entertain you'
It was so loud that Grandad had to block his ears
A diva match!
One skinny fit lady skipped into the ring
The crowd cheered!
One fat lady like a sumo strutted into the ring
The crowd booed!
The fit lady won.

Then there was a Royal Rumble
The first wrestler went out; it was the Yank American,
He got clotheslined over the ropes onto the announcer's table.
Robbie the Scouser raised his arms in triumph
The noise was deafening
The people piled in to join in kicking the cheating wrestlers
                                      as they came over the ropes
The whole night was cool.

Jamie McLaughlan (11)
Northern House School (BESD), Oxford

Through The Eyes Of A Battery Hen

Same seed again, through the bars again,
Wish there was something different.
Where is the grass
And why is it so cramped in here?
My feet hurt.
I wish, I wish I could sit in a field, just for a moment.
To play with the other chickens in the sun,
To feel the sun on my feathers would be like a dream.
What's that banging on the roof?
I hope it's something to get us out,
Maybe it's that thing called rain.
Oh no, it's the humans, not me, I thought I'd laid enough eggs
                                              this time,

Phew! They cooked Clucky.

Mitchel Why (12)
Northern House School (BESD), Oxford

The Life Of My Friend Rachel

Rachel is sometimes angry
When she's bossy and frustrated and hot.
She looks very calm and happy too.
Rachel is always helpful to you.
She's nice but has lost her temper a thousand times.
She gets very upset when somebody teases her,
As upset as anyone can be, as you see.
But she likes us and is always friends with me.

Alysia Bradbrook-Armit (14)
Penn School, Penn

What Is My Purpose In Life?

In the world hunters hunt and kill animals,
It's usually for their fur or tusks or horns.
Some hunters usually hunt animals for sport,
Animals lose their mothers like Bambi the fawn.
People pollute our oceans with oil,
The pollution kills all the sea creatures.
There are other types of pollution that spoil
The oceans and kill the fish and whales.
I want to stop this before it's too late
Or all the animals will die.

This will be my purpose in life.

Michael Kane (14)
Penn School, Penn

Why I Am Here

Why I am here to make people beautiful?
Why I am here to put colour in people's hair.
Why I am here to cut hair in styles.
Why I am here to paint your nails.
Why I am here to make you shine.
You are stunning, let me help you.
Why I am here to make your hair glow.
Why I am here to make your nails sparkly.
That's why I am here.

Ravneet Janda (15)
Penn School, Penn

Angels

True angels help you up when you are down.
True angels never let you do something that you'll regret the next day.
True angels keep promises and share.
True angels are always by your side or close to your heart.
True angels understand, believe and support you when times
are tough.
Look around you, you're surrounded by angels, they're your
best friends.

Lisa Ward (15)
Penn School, Penn

Blind Man's Buff

You think I can cope,
But I can't.
You think I don't care,
Well, I do.
You think I'm not sad,
Well, I am.
You think it's not dark,
Well, it is.
You think I'm not scared,
Well, you're wrong.
You think I'm so clumsy,
Well, you're right.
You think I'm so independent,
I wish I was.
You think I don't miss your face,
Well, I do.
You think I can play games,
Well, I can't.
You think I can't read,
Well, I'd love to.
You think I like taxis,
I'd rather drive.
Do you think blind is fun?
Well, it isn't.

James Pervoe (15)
Penn School, Penn

One Thing Needful

Words thrown get seized with ears
Grasping tight
Then thrown hard and far away
The listener was the future
Convinced of the powers of change
Doesn't need your help

Words float back gracefully
Like the repetition taught in English
With rolled eyes the words are missed
Not seen or heard
Repetition of misinformation is concentrated
There was possibility of a great future
The great possibility of achievement in those eyes
It is missed
No help is needed

Perseverance stands close by
It has returned
Never giving up
Trying to teach its qualities
Desired but rejected
It has failed to pass on
'Do you need help?'
No, it's not needed

Determination has kept the company of perseverance
Attacking the heart
Weakening
Strengthening
Making way for lessons and perseverance
Determined to make positive life experiences
Through the education of self
The recognition of the need for help
Do you need any help?

Nwadiogo Quartey-Ngwube (18)
Rye Saint Antony School, Headington

Broken World

Fear, suffering, bloodshed, murder, war, terrorism.
How much further will we go to become victorious?
Poverty, famine, illness, death.
How many people will breathe their last breath
Because of this nightmare?
But then somewhere amidst the depression and fear,
A smiling face will bring happiness near
And peace, I hope, shall reign.

It shall call to the people, 'Come one, come all!
Hear this message of love and life.
Let poverty and warfare cease
And love and forgiveness rule.'

And creatures great and small
And humans short and tall
Shall come together as one
To mend this broken world.

But until that fateful day should come
We live in fear,
But know this reader, you may find comfort
In the knowledge of what you have read.
The world will not always be broken.

Katharine Eakin (12)
St Leonards-Mayfield School, Mayfield

The Journey

Waiting for the chairlift to take me up, up, up
Look behind! Here it comes; jump on, quick, pull the bar down,
Don't drop my poles.
Phew! Safely sitting on the chairlift.

People skiing below me,
Some tall, some small, some fast, some slow.
People tumbling head over heels, skis falling, off poles
                                      flying everywhere.

Higher into the mountains I go, above the tall green pine trees,
Getting colder, it's starting to snow.
Large snowflakes on my goggles, I can see my warm breath
                                      in the cold air,
Snow swirling all around me.

Nearly at the top of the lift, the white slopes below me,
Get ready, lift the bar, there we go, jump off, don't fall over.
Phew! Safely off and on my skis.

Everybody's ready, off we go, let's race.
Zoom down the mountain; avoid skiers ahead, jumping jumps,
Zigzagging from side to side,
Don't fall over!
Back at the bottom, all in one piece,
Time for a mug of hot chocolate.

Olivia Mills (12)
St Leonards-Mayfield School, Mayfield

My Grandma

My grandma is a shrivelled-up prune,
She never knows who's in the room.
My mummy says she's only blind,
But Daddy says she's lost her mind!
She walks about all tattered and torn
With a look on her face all sad and forlorn.
She croaks and groans and pokes and moans,
'And in my day . . .' on and on she drones.
Her memory is fading, quite quickly if I may say
But I love my grandma with all my heart,
It's hell watching her decay.

Olivia Cottrell (12)
St Leonards-Mayfield School, Mayfield

A Fit Of Nerves

Butterflies fluttering in the stomach
A feeling of weakness in the knees,
Giving way, colour sapping from the cheeks
Until I am as pale and ephemeral as a ghost.
Heavy feet glued to the floor,
The brain frozen with fear,
Ears turn deaf, voices muffle
Was that my name being called?
I respond like a robot with sudden anxiety
Was that my name being summoned to the stage to sing my solo?
The notes begin to trouble me.
How will I remember and will my voice perform?
Will that sea of faces strike me with terror?
I stand on stage and wait as silence overawes the room.
A nod from my teacher prompting me to begin.
My mouth opens, my voice cracks like a loudspeaker
                with volume uncontrolled.
I blurt out the title . . .
And when the piece is over, that I can't remember saying,
Still numb, the crowd applauds, my knees shake
Blindly, I return to my seat
And the butterflies vanish with my relief.

Elinor Bushell (11)
St Leonards-Mayfield School, Mayfield

Sudden End

What is happening?
We've suddenly stopped moving.
People are screaming, running far away.
Like a toy, we plunged to the ground
And we're definitely not going to our destination today.

Wild flames flicker, glass has smashed,
Burnt seats and suitcases crushed poor passengers.
There is a man; he was sitting next to me
And now is on the floor, screaming in agony.
My journey has crashed to a halt and so
I don't know whether my life has too.
Cruising through the air, then suddenly in ruins
The plane's life has gone and mine is going soon.

Vicci Cowlett (13)
St Mary's Hall School, Brighton

Dolphin

The dolphin swims like a playful child
It dives into the ocean waves
Like a sleek streamlined swimmer
He splashes his tail powerfully
And somersaults and tumbles gracefully
Under the almighty push of the waves
Until his fins will swim no more
Which is when he dives into the deep blue sea
Where the eyes of people cannot see.

Sam Jordan (13)
The Buckingham Secondary School, Buckingham

Grandma Elizabeth

You were beautiful
You were careful
There for Mum
Every single day.

I love you and want you
Need you and trust you
Everything you went through
I am so proud of you.

Where have you gone?
You're always in my mind
More always in your heart
With me every day.

In every single way
Push me out of harm's way
We raised money for you
And everyone likes you.
I love you Grandma
Oh where are you?

Siân Mason (12)
The Buckingham Secondary School, Buckingham

You Light Up My World

I think about you every day
I love you more than words can say.
Every day in the park
I see you and your friend have a laugh.
I love the way that you talk
But then again I love your walk.
Every day since the first day of school
I've always thought you're really cool.
Every night I hate to think you're not beside me
You light up my world.

Bryony Foote (12)
The Buckingham Secondary School, Buckingham

Bunny Love

When I bounce I see you there
You hop like me without a care.
Your fur is soft as a newly pulled-out carrot
With love in the middle of each.
You make me laugh when you shake your tail
But when I dance I always fail.
I love the way you walk like an angel
To me you can fly without fail.
I love you more than a bunch of carrots
You're the one, you're my little bunny.

Olivia Venables (11)
The Buckingham Secondary School, Buckingham

Love

When I see your eyes
They make me want to fly
Up to the sky
Then you walk right by
I really love you
And I know that you do.
Please give me strength
So that I can go to the length
This was all for you
This wasn't cool
This was all for you
Now it's the end
Now it's time for the doves
To say goodbye to my love.

Daniel Mills (11)
The Buckingham Secondary School, Buckingham

He Is Here

In the park,
In the dark,
In the rain,
Feeling pain
Because he's here.

On the ice,
Roll the dice,
Is there a chance
I'll survive?
Because, he's here.

Sitting on a fence,
The air is usually dense,
Look behind,
He's not very kind,
He's here.

A street light turns on,
Is this all just a con,
Look around to see him and
Argh!

Archie Keir (12)
The Buckingham Secondary School, Buckingham

The Perfect Dog

Begin with bags full of happiness
This will make the mixture sweet.
Add a teaspoon of softness and an ounce of fluffiness
Mixed with cuteness for added cuddliness.
Next stir in jet-black colour or puppy-brown eyes
In order to make it look sweet.
Bake for fifteen years
And serve with a long walk on the beach.

Becky Fowler (13)
The Buckingham Secondary School, Buckingham

Love

He filled his fingers with mine,
He called me his baby,
He took me at my worst
But he still said I was beautiful.
Our memories I will never forget,
Our first kiss was everything,
I said I will never hurt him,
I said I will always love him
And I promised him that.
These three little words mean so much
I love you!
But how can this be? I feel so happy
I've never felt this feeling over someone before,
But I like it.
These two wrords are the ones for me,
In love.

Jodie Taylor (12)
The Buckingham Secondary School, Buckingham

Dreams

Am I already asleep? Is this it?
Will I not wake up for a bright summer's day?
Am I already asleep dreaming of dreams?
Dreams can be lonely, dreams can be scary
But the dream I'm in is not a dream, it's a nightmare!
All alone in this cold dark place, will I wake up or am I awake?
But when you are asleep you can't feel real pain but I do!
Why do I cry and feel the cold tears run down my face?
So many questions and so little answers,
Why is it that the questions you need answered
                              are the questions that aren't?
Dreams, dreams.
Maybe I'm alone forever,
Maybe I'm in a dream,
Maybe I'm in a nightmare,
I felt my eyes open, I was in a hospital
I was in a coma there were people who were in my dream
Am I awake or is this still a dream?

Leah Robinson (13)
The Buckingham Secondary School, Buckingham

My Love For You

I think about you all the time
I think of you in English, French and music.
When I am lying in bed I think that you are next to me.
I thought I saw you smile at me.
Whenever I hear you talk, my knees go weak.
When I see you smile you melt my heart.
I love the sound of your name.
When I look at the gaps between my hands
I want your hands to fill the gaps.
I love you so much.
I wish you were all mine.

Leanne Mayhew (12)
The Buckingham Secondary School, Buckingham

Questions

Questions and questions keep going through my head
Wondering whether my mum is dead.
Childhood memory left on a door,
A teardrop fall is all I saw.
Mum, Mum, where are you?
Come back for me and we can move.
Together forever we could be
But only if you come for me.
Questions, questions I need to know
Is she here, someone help me so.
Mum come home, don't leave me alone,
I have my questions, please let me know.

Hannah Brinn (13)
The Buckingham Secondary School, Buckingham

The Perfect Relationship

Begin with bags full of love
This will make the mixture sweet.
Add a teaspoon of romance and add an ounce of trust
Mix with feelings for each other for added true love.
Next stir in a Valentine's card or a box of chocolates
In order to keep the love alive.
Bake for your lifetime and serve with marriage and happy times.

StaceyLeigh Dalton (12)
The Buckingham Secondary School, Buckingham

The Perfect Recipe For A Class

First you add a spoonful of Jodie
A tint of Ryan
Mix the flour with the Sam
Then add the Kyle and the Becky
Why not add some Stacey
Cut up the Hannah and mix in the Leanne
Then put in the Dani
Add the jam and the Leah
Cut the Liam in half
And add it with Jess
And put in the Harriett
And put it in the oven
For the temperature of the class.

Harriet Mitchell (13)
The Buckingham Secondary School, Buckingham

Everything In This World Seems Black And White

Black and white faces
Black and white places
Everything seems black and white to me
Dim and lonely
I just can't find myself
It's just so colourless
The hair
The face
The clothing
The place
I was born in
Is so black and white
It never changes
It's like we're in cages
Black and white
It never feels right
Soundless
They can't hear the screams
From my bedroom where as a little girl I used to lie and dream
Everything is colourless after that day
I just wish it would colour up one day again.

Megan Bainbridge (13)
The Buckingham Secondary School, Buckingham

Pain Of Global Warming

Slow, the way I go
Fast the way I think
Wondering whether life will end
Or if we all sink
Slow the way we are drowning
Fast the way we sleep
Wondering whether we scream or weep

Slow the way we get away
Fast the way there's no other way
Knowing life is gone today
Slow the way your mother sighs
Fast the way your father cries
Wondering whoever dies

Slow the way we have no escape
Fast the way we try and create
Wondering if we'll calm this down
Or if we're dying and to drown

Slow the way we swim away
Fast the way we'll never stay
Knowing life is now at its end
Crying, worried, as this isn't pretend.

Polly Mullins (12)
The Buckingham Secondary School, Buckingham

The Floorboards

Sat in my room
On a cold winter's night
Under the covers
Came such a fright.
The thunder was loud
And I saw a huge cloud
That loomed over my bed
Then got stuck on my head!
These big floorboard creatures
Came out through the night
They smacked nails into my head.
I fell over and a knife went in my back
I told my insurance company and they didn't give me jack.
So now I am sitting here alone and poor
My mummy and daddy fell through the floor
And the moral of the poem is
Don't trust floorboard people, they make you kiss.

Ryan Critoph (13)
The Buckingham Secondary School, Buckingham

The Funeral

No sense of smell
No one to tell
Fingers numb and cold
As the secrets unfold

A hole in the ground
I was once lost then found
But now I'm in a hole
I hide all alone

My soul mate, my lover
There was never any other
I love you my dear
And for the future I fear.

Josie Swindell (12)
The Buckingham Secondary School, Buckingham

She Was Gone

We were walking,
We were talking,
She pointed her finger down the road.
I looked over my shoulder,
Nothing was there,
I turned back towards her,
She was gone,
She was gone.
I looked around me,
She was gone,
She was gone.
Then I saw,
Down by my feet,
There she lay,
Motionless and in pain.
She stared up towards me
And squealed, 'Do, I do!'
Before I could move a muscle,
She closed her eyes,
She was gone,
She was gone,
Now I wonder what she meant by, 'Do, I do!'

Jasmin Stevens (11)
The Buckingham Secondary School, Buckingham

Not Smiling But Dying

Nobody heard me, the invisible girl,
Inside I was screaming
To let my true self out,
Not smiling but dying.

Loneliness was a stone in my heart,
Desperate, I tried to rip it out
But it was a part of me,
It would never go, there was no doubt.

I would always be bleeding,
Friendships gradually seeping out of my mind,
I would be all alone,
Too far out to be kind.

At least that's how it seemed
Until a friend came running,
Who was suffering just like me,
Not smiling but living.

Katrina Lambert (13)
The Buckingham Secondary School, Buckingham

Not An Orphan's World

I sit on the broken spring bed
Watching New York go by,
I hate this world, I hate my life,
So now I'm going to die.

They don't know me, none of them do,
They are all perfectly loved,
Nobody notices me anyway
So they won't even know if I'm gone.

I dream of a new life,
A dream without despair,
I dream of great happiness
But I'm alone and no one is there.

Now New York is at my feet,
It's time to spread my wings,
The wind blowing through my hair,
The Devil takes what an angel brings.

Ellen Whitbread (12)
The Buckingham Secondary School, Buckingham

The Monster's Wish

I wish I was as free as the wild horses
That canter through the open land,
As wild or loud as the wind
That whips through their home.

I wish I could laugh and love
Without being laughed at or killed,
But this is life and there's no wishing in life,
There's only sadness.

So as you wanted me a killer,
You will get me as a killer
And no one can tame me,
That you will see.

Nicola George (12)
The Buckingham Secondary School, Buckingham

Friendless

I don't know why they go for me,
I don't do anything, I let them be.
If this one girl didn't exist,
I could have had the chance to make new friends.

They stare and laugh then turn away,
I wake up thinking, *what's going to happen today?*
I stand and wait for me to be picked,
Though I'm always last, no team wants me.

What's wrong with me, can someone say?
I'm trapped in a game that I can't play,
They wait for me at the corner, take the mick
Then throw me away like rubbish.

What's wrong with me I say again?
Where can I go for help?
I'm scared of them I know I shouldn't be,
I should tell, but who's there for me?

Three years from now, looking back,
From how it used to be,
I told someone it all worked out,
And now they're friends with me.

Anna Cresswell (12)
The Buckingham Secondary School, Buckingham

Outsider

An outsider always gets hurt
An outsider is always different
An outsider always belongs in its own place
But an outsider is always normal.

Olie Newton (12)
The Buckingham Secondary School, Buckingham

Why I Won't Go Home!
(Based on 'Secrets' by Jacqueline Wilson)

He unbuckled his heavy leather belt!
'She needs teaching a lesson once and for all!'
Mum tried to laugh him out of it,
but when he raised his belt I felt ever so small.

Mum yelled at me to run for it!
'Don't let him hit you with his belt!
Because you feel deep pain,
that in the past I have felt.'

Mum cried, Bethany cried, Kyle cried too,
blood trickled down in my eyes as I found.
I stared straight at his cold green eyes,
if only I was with Nan, I'd be safe and sound.

I wonder what will happen next.
I wonder if it will leave a scar.
I don't want to know right now
I just want to go away to Grandma's car.

Eunice Ngala (11)
The Buckingham Secondary School, Buckingham

The Lonely Orphan

The boy sits alone in a cold dark room
With only rats for comfort
And the sense he keeps feeling is the sense of doom
When he looks down at his scars and bruises

He lies on a cold broken bed
With only a window for light
And as he watches the cars go by
He wonders will his life ever be as good as that

His dreams are only the other side of his door
And as willing as he is to go out there
He never dares to go near it
Because he is scared of his angry father

He wonders shall he risk the torture and pain
As he has never seen the outside of his room
As he walks towards the door
He can see shadows from under it

He reaches for the cold metal handle
And as he turns it he hears a loud scream and then nothing happens
He jumps and runs back to his bed
Two years later
Alone in his room
No one has seen him
No one knows him; he is just a lonely sad orphan.

Abby Ramanauckis (12)
The Buckingham Secondary School, Buckingham

A Drop From My Eye

It all went so quick
I thought it was a trick
The stench of death
A drip, a drop from my eye
The love of my grandad gone for life

Nothing left but the thoughts of his life
Rocking back and forth on his old armchair
I will never forget the warmth of his palms

To know the immoral smoking habits
Led him to his death bed, I don't want to think about it
But I will never forget the smile on his face when I walked in the room
He's dead, I'm scarred for life.

Ben Ogle (12)
The Buckingham Secondary School, Buckingham

A Snowy Day

Feather-light snow had fallen during the day
The grass was being suffocated by a carpet of white.
Children sprung into their wellies
And wrapped up warm ready to make footsteps around the white lawn.
The children had a snowball fight but before they knew it, day
                                        had turned to night.
At night the snow was freezing which was very unpleasing.
The sun came out the next day and melted all the snow away.

Hattie Jeffs (11)
The Buckingham Secondary School, Buckingham

Little Red

Poor old Gran
Sick in bed,
I'll take her some wine
And give her some bread.

I went down the road
Wrapped in my cloak,
I reached her house
All alone, no folk.

I banged on the door
Here's someone wrapped in a shawl,
There stood a figure
Not Gran at all!

Great big eyes,
Big ears
And paws,
Imagine how much
Fear was caused.

I tried to run
But she ate me for tea,
But the axe man came
And set me free!

Rhiannon Taylor (11)
The Buckingham Secondary School, Buckingham

No Answer

No calls from him today,
No messages from him I say,
No answer.

I called him on the landline,
No answer.

I checked my answering machine,
No answer.

I called him on his secret mobile,
No answer.

I knocked on his front door,
No answer.

I threw a rock at his window,
No answer.

Strange!
Strange!
Really strange!

I broke into his house, nearly shocked to my death.
Now I know there will never be an answer from
My love, my love, my love,
My love has . . . no answer.

D'Maria Fernander (11)
The Buckingham Secondary School, Buckingham

Perfect Outfit

Begin with lingerie
Add a mini skirt
Then an ounce of leggings
Mix with a T-shirt and a jumper too
Sprinkle on some jewellery
Stir in some dolly shoes
And serve with a bow.

Ashleigh-Rose Turner (13)
The Buckingham Secondary School, Buckingham

Friendship

Ashleigh is my friend
But she drives me round the bend.
Joe is pretty cool
But he likes to call me a fool

My friend is Polly
She thinks she's a dolly.
James is wicked
And his dad is called Sid.

Friendship you should treasure
If you leave, your friends will miss ya.
My class is all right
Even though Laura likes to bite.

I wouldn't want to give it away
That is all I have to say.
I'm running out of paper
So see ya later.

Andrew Brooker (12)
The Buckingham Secondary School, Buckingham

In An English Lesson

In an English lesson
It is as exciting as the jungle
Miss Gibb shouting as loud as a lion's roar
With Lizzy and Ashleigh being so annoying
Tom Clarke as quiet as a mouse

Andrew thinking he's Vicky Pollard
Laura thinking she is well hard
Jack chatting all the time
Benito and Alex thinking they're so clever
But I am never.

Joe Townsend (12)
The Buckingham Secondary School, Buckingham

My Dog

My dog is like a black and white fur ball
When she hears the word, 'Walkies'
My dog is like a crazy madman
Running in front of cars.

My dog goes mad at the colour silver
And her pink lead
My dog is a daredevil
Riding on a motorbike.
Some people are scared of my dog
Some people think she is fun
My sister likes our dog
I think our dog is number one.

Our dog's name is Amy
With her fluffy fur
But we just like our dog
When she is just her.

Alex Price (12)
The Buckingham Secondary School, Buckingham

Word Of Warning

Please do not go to Spain
Or your house will get knocked down by a crane.
Please do not go to Iran
You might get blown up, you stupid man!
Please do not go to Ghana
Because I heard there's poison in the lasagne.
Please do not go to Japan
You could meet a bloke called the Chainsaw Man.
Please do not go to New York
You might get stabbed with a bloody pitchfork.
Please do not go to Ibiza,
When I last went there they put worms in my pizza.
Please do not go to visit the sea
You might get infected by a toddler's wee.
Please do not go to Sardinia
You will probably catch a bad case of double pneumonia.
Please do not go to Poland
You could meet a maniac called Phillip J Rowland.
Please do not go to Wales
You will get addicted to the bargain sales.
Please do not go to France
Because that's where all the naked ladies dance.

Jack Reynolds (13)
The Buckingham Secondary School, Buckingham

My Love

My love is like a bird
Soaring through the air
People always make fun of me
But I don't really care.

My love for her is really strong
Strong enough to pull through
We'll never be in the wrong.

My love for her will never fade
I'll love her for days and days
If she doesn't love me that's OK
We'll be together forever, every single day.

George Chisholme (12)
The Buckingham Secondary School, Buckingham

NSPCC

Hand marks across my face
Feeling so out of place
He made me feel a big disgrace.

Pushed up against the wall
He is big and tall
Look at me I'm short and small.

Bruises on my back
Happiness is what I lack
Tied up on a train track.

Scars upon my dainty arm
My brain flashes like an alarm
Trying to keep myself steady and clam.

Beaten, battered, betrayed and bashed
These things can stop with your cash
Donate to the NSPCC now
And the child you saw will be in good company.

Emma Curley (12)
The Buckingham Secondary School, Buckingham

Tears

I cry when I remember
The only reason you left was because of her
I wake up in the morning and cry
Because I realise it's another day without you by my side
If she hadn't lied, well, there would be tears I wouldn't have cried.

Jennifer Mepham (13)
The Buckingham Secondary School, Buckingham

Feeling

The sound of waves drift me to sleep
While the night sky lurks in the air
The sound of humming from the shells
And the softness on my feet
Feels like I'm in Heaven
Now you know my feelings
Tell me yours.

Aisha Thornton (12)
The Buckingham Secondary School, Buckingham

Bullies

B eing mean
U nkind
L osing grip
L aughter no more
I t scares me
E very day
S omeday it will end.

Samantha Holder (13)
The Buckingham Secondary School, Buckingham

What Is It?

I'm not quite sure what,
I'm not quite sure when,
But there's something underneath my bed!

Is it a spider?
Is it a mat?
Is it something dead or flat?

Every time I see it, it makes me feel sick
It just appeared there, it's never been there before.
I don't want to touch it,
What is it?

Kimberley Price (13)
The Buckingham Secondary School, Buckingham

Love

Love is a moment
A moment in life
Where you get a feeling
Deep down inside
When your dream boy
You've always liked
Rides along on his
Multicoloured bike
You think for a moment
And stop and stare
When you glance and see
His short brown hair.
Love is something special
Each and every day
Whilst little children are playing
The big boys come out and play.

Joanne Higgins (13)
The Buckingham Secondary School, Buckingham

Wolves

You're walking home through the woods
When you hear a cracking sound.
At first you think nothing of it
Then you hear a growl.
You turn around to see what's there
But there's nothing to be found.
Then you hear it again, this time very loud
It's definitely getting closer and it's sounding very cross
You decide the time has come to run but you slip on the moss.
The footsteps are just behind you, you dare not to peep
You bury your head in the ground and realise you were just asleep!

Zach Campbell (13)
The Buckingham Secondary School, Buckingham

My War Life

My body trembling with fear
My arms, stiff as twigs
My bones creaking like floorboards
My fingers shaking like an earthquake.

The Germans are getting closer
What should I do?
The Germans are getting closer
Should I bomb them or shoot?

Bang! goes the rifle
Another mate down dead
The Nazis have shot him
And now I am scared.

The Germans are much closer
Another mate down dead
The Germans are much closer
Should I run or should I stay?

I reach for my shotgun
I try to blast his head
But the silly little German
Shot me down instead!

Ben Baker (13)
The Buckingham Secondary School, Buckingham

Under The Sea

Under the sea there's
Fish,
Starfish,
Shells and more,
There's crabs, let's go and grab them
If we can.

Under the sea there are
Octopus which have eight legs for eight different things,
Cooking,
Spying,
Eating,
Moving,
Stealing
Swimming,
Keeping safe,
And protecting friends.

Under the sea there are
Dolphins,
Sharks, *argh!*
Sharks will bite,
Sharks will eat,
So watch out, keep an eye on your feet

Under the sea there are
Whales,
Jellyfish,
Swordfish,
Watch out, don't get sawn in half.
Keep your body together
Under the sea!

Kirsty Barson (13)
The Buckingham Secondary School, Buckingham

Where's My Mouse?

'Mum, I've lost my mouse again.'
'Oh you silly boy, go look for him.'
I ran upstairs to check the rooms
First I went to check my room
I checked the bed, then the shelf,
But did not see him on the books.
I checked the wardrobe then the box
I'm going to get told off, oh my God!
I checked the living room hoping he would be there
Seeing the cat made me more scared.
I checked its mouth then its paws,
No, it's not there, it's somewhere else.
I checked the kitchen and in the cooker
No, it's not there, *ouch!* I burnt my finger.
Mum came up to me, 'Found him yet?'
'No I have not Mum, I think he's gone.'
'Dear have you checked your jumper yet?'
'No, why would he have got in there?'
I searched my pocket and found something fluffy,
Oh I'm so stupid, he's always been there.

Sophie Carr (12)
The Buckingham Secondary School, Buckingham

Babies

When you find out something,
Something truly amazing,
To know that in your heart
You have made something wonderful.
And that something is a baby.
A baby growing inside you
Growing an arm or a leg
Your stomach getting much bigger.

Then you decide on names,
What shall I call my baby?
What if it's a boy?
What if it's a girl?

Then you start to buy things
You tell your family,
You show your family,
Then your friends gets the news.

It comes out as a boy,
That boy gets called Thomas.
The clothes you bought get worn,
The things you bought get used.

As the days pass, your child gets older, it starts to smile,
That one baby can bring so much joy; it's so amazing to think
You made the most wonderful thing in the world!

Gemma Chittenden (13)
The Buckingham Secondary School, Buckingham

Animals

Little snails on the wall
Which little snails shall I choose?
Snails too big, snails too small,
Please can you give me some little clues?

Spiders, spiders, little creepy spiders
Run up and down their little sticky webs.
Crush and squish those little creepy spiders
So they don't disturb me in my comfy bed.

Little worms on the path,
Sliding along on the little bits of grass.
Which little worm should I bury in the grass
So I can try to find it with my magnifying glass?

William Edmondson (12)
The Buckingham Secondary School, Buckingham

Birds Poem

Some are small and some are big
Some fly up high, some fly down low
Some like the city and some like the country
But always are seen to be quite hungry.
Some like trees, some like buildings
Some fly fast, some fly slow
And some prefer to stay down low.

Others hide and others seek
Others prefer just to peek
And others like to creep and creep
Until they are caught
Then they would have thought
I should have came a different way
Or should I have decided to stay?

Luke Hancock (12)
The Buckingham Secondary School, Buckingham

Winter's Gone

Winter's going, plants are growing
The trees have got their leaves back
There's cold in the air but the sun's on the way
The winter has flown on by.
Buy some suncream; go on holiday to where you've never been before
Go to a gig or two while the sky is still blue
Enjoy a ride in your convertible with your hair blowing back
Winter's gone, so just relax.

Leanne Day (13)
The Buckingham Secondary School, Buckingham

The Motorway

I'm travelling down the motorway in my car
I'm driving to a place not too far.
There's a car in front, I'm gaining too fast,
Indicate left, right in front of a speeding lorry!
I begin to speed up, straight into the back of a slow-moving truck.
I think myself lucky; I wonder what happened to the girl in the buggy?
At the side of the road, I dial the code,
They say it'll be fine, but I know it won't in the back of my mind.
So whatever you do, be careful out there,
You're lucky, you're here today reading my poem.

Andrew Kebbell (12)
The Buckingham Secondary School, Buckingham

Why Daddy?

Why do you have grey hair Dad?
Why do you have hair under your nose?
Why don't I have grey hair Dad?
Why don't you smell like a rose?

Why can't I have a dog Dad?
Why are you so bad at golf?
Why are you taller than Mum, Dad?
Why am I so good at golf?

Why are you so good at footie Dad?
Why do we have a blue car?
Why are you so funny Dad?
Why play golf when you are over par?

Why do you drive so fast Dad?
Why do you have nice clubs?
Why are you a builder Dad?
Why do you drink in pubs?

Ben Oliver (12)
The Buckingham Secondary School, Buckingham

Deforestation

Down goes one tree, there goes another,
I reckon that one was his little brother.
Down go the trees one by one,
Soon how many will be left? Absolutely none!
I want to stop this, what can I do?
They might lock me up and maybe you too.
But I want to stop all this deforestation
It's causing the animals' pain and frustration.
So what can I do?
Will you help me save all the forests too?

Matthew Shackell (12)
The Buckingham Secondary School, Buckingham

This Is All Because Of That Silly Cat!

This area is getting spooky
I can't believe I'm loopy
This is really getting hot
So I think I will blow my top
I think this is getting darker
So I push the button harder
I've just seen a ghost
So I'm going to boast
Don't tell me why
Otherwise I will cry
I slipped on the floor
Broke the door
Then there was no more of that
I will always blame that silly cat!

Ben Phillips (12)
The Buckingham Secondary School, Buckingham

Chocolate

I was meant to ration
I have one confession
I fell to temptation
I have a question
Why do I love chocolate?
I need a lesson
To control my obsession
I lost my domination
I need ammunition
I still don't know.

Benjamin Rowell (13)
The Buckingham Secondary School, Buckingham

The Normal School Day

What did you learn at school?
My bag fell in the swimming pool
Went to lesson, it was great
Apart from the fact that I was late
Science, English, geography
They are all the best for me
Went to the office today
But they sent me straight away
My mum rang to say she's late
So I went home with a mate.

Kayleigh Honor (13)
The Buckingham Secondary School, Buckingham

Animal Wood

Cold in the night, oh what a fright
Walking through the woods late one night.
The cries of foxes, the hoot of owls
The growls of badgers, oh what a row!

I stay standing here shivering in my boots
Oh what was that?
It was only a big black cat.
'What are you doing here?' I asked
'Miaow,' it replied, 'You should not be out on this cold dark night
You gave me a fright you poor little mite
Please don't bite, it will soon be light.'

I sat down closing my eyes
The cat lay beside me, no one else in sight,
Goodnight.

Tom Reading (13)
The Buckingham Secondary School, Buckingham

Running

We are both useless at racing
Me and my friend,
Slow at the start
Dead slow at the end.

I get a stitch
She gets sore feet,
So none of us ever complete.

But however cooperation
A total different case
You should see us
In the three-legged race!

Tate Butler (13)
The Buckingham Secondary School, Buckingham

Paper Boy

I am a paper boy
I do a paper round,
Whenever I do it,
I fall on the ground.
I deliver the mail
And my face goes pale.
It's so cold
I could go bold.
I wear my thermal stuff
Otherwise I feel rough.

Jack Carpenter (13)
The Buckingham Secondary School, Buckingham

Drugs

It isn't cool and it isn't funny
It will cost you loads of money
All your dreams going down the drain
Are you crazy or just insane?

You can answer that question on your own
You probably won't be living in a home
Do you think you're clever? Do you think you're funny?
You'll be the one without any money!

You're probably be living on the street
You'll probably won't have any shoes on your feet
Because you're so desperate
You won't know what to do
You'll buy drugs to get you through.

Jonathon Clark (12)
The Buckingham Secondary School, Buckingham

Cries Of The World

Our world
What has it come to?
What have we done?

War faces every corner of the globe
Forest destroyed to make things like wardrobes
Death spread all over the land
These drugs are destroying you, don't you understand?

Pollution threatening the ozone
While people lie in the streets all alone
Terrorists destroy without a care for the world
While terrified parents cry for their kidnapped girl.

Crime is rising every day
All we can do is pray for it to be okay
Extinct animals all over the land
Countries invaded because of high oil demand.

The world is crying out for people to see
What has been done but wasn't meant to be
Ignorance has crowded many people's lives
But all the world can do is cry, cry, cry.

Dean Faulkner (13)
The Buckingham Secondary School, Buckingham

Animal

A nimals are cute
N ature involves lots of different animals
I n everyone's dreams
M ad and funny
A musing creatures
L oving and caring.

Abbie Livingstone (11)
The Buckingham Secondary School, Buckingham

Shopping

I'm in the car in my best jeans
Really excited about this shopping spree
We'll go to BHS, Tammy and New Look
Maybe even Ottakers to buy a new book.
We get out of the car walk through the double doors
Up the stairs to the top floor.
This top, these trousers, I must have it all
But then I found out they were a size too small!
Four bags I carried into KFC
Chicken wings, some chips and a drink for me.
Yum-yum, I eat it all up
'Any seconds?'
'No thanks, I've had enough!'

Hannah Biltcliffe (11)
The Buckingham Secondary School, Buckingham

Life

Life is like a river
Flowing, flowing down stream
As you flow you visit new places and different faces.

Life is like a journey
A long, long journey
The journey can lead you anywhere.

Life is like a roller coaster
Rolling and rolling
There are highs and there are lows.

Life is like a school
Forever overloading your brain with ideas
You learn new things as you move on.

What do you think of life?

Josh Hill (11)
The Buckingham Secondary School, Buckingham

Up The Stairs

So big, so steep but up it shall be,
Climbing it,
Jumping it,
Running it,
But how shall I do it?
The last step, I have to do it,
Now, to go down . . . but how?

Sebastian Holuj (12)
The Buckingham Secondary School, Buckingham

A Poem About My Cat Bungle

I have a cat called Bungle
He is completely grey
And if a dog chases him
He would run away.
He runs around the house
Like a little rat,
He goes into the hallway
And starts to scratch the mat.
Bungle has really fluffy cheeks
And when my mum's cooking,
He goes and peeks.
Bungle has really green eyes
He is strange because he likes pies.
When he is angry he starts to wag his tail
If you hurt him he will start to wail.
Bungle is really kind
Because when you're blue
He will speak, miaow, while he's creeping up behind
And he will lick you.
Bungle's fur is bluey-grey and curly
When I stroke him he is so adorable and furry.
When you pick him up and he doesn't like it
He will go all floppy or have a fit.
If something scares him, his eyes will go big and wide
Also he would run away and hide.
His fur would go all fuzzy
He will chase anything buzzy.
So that's all from Bungle and me
Until next time, he'll be under a tree.

Rebecca Eggleton (11)
The Buckingham Secondary School, Buckingham

The Boneless Snake

Here and there I go
Slithering on my body
Seeing humans everywhere
Wishing I had bones
So I could walk on my toes
Feeling full of shame
Here I slither all alone
Like a train with no one inside
Oh, I wish I had bones.

Kar Yeun Tang (12)
The Buckingham Secondary School, Buckingham

The Homeless Dog

Here I lie in the rain
In so much pain,
I hope my owner comes back one day
Because still here I lay.
In the cold
This life is ever so bold,
I would give anything to eat
But no, I'm still lying on this car seat.
My mind is a swirl
Just like this messed-up world.

Billy Jones (12)
The Buckingham Secondary School, Buckingham

I Am A . . .

I am a book with no pictures
But with a good front cover
I am an object with many words
With three hundred pages.
I am a dog sitting in my bed
People keep asking me questions
But I don't know what they want.
I am a toothbrush waiting to be used
I only get used twice a day that is not enough.
I am a bar of chocolate, smooth and chewy, everyone likes me,
I am addictive like a packet of cigarettes
I am tastier though I'm sure!

Dominic Dunn (12)
The Buckingham Secondary School, Buckingham

A Classroom's Day

I know I'm a springy chair
And I am always bare,
I huff and I huff until I go puff
When people sit on me.

I know I'm a boring old table
And people lean on me,
I'm not cared for, plus it's not fair
When people lean on me.

I know I'm a sad clean light
And I shine all day,
I wait and I wait until I go *pop*
When people turn me off.

I know I'm a black dusty blind
And I go up and down,
I stop and I stop the sun coming in
When people don't love me.

I know I'm a worn, used classroom
And I see different people a day
I look and I look till I am bored
When people learn in me.

Rebecca Blackmore (12)
The Buckingham Secondary School, Buckingham

The New One

My mummy does not understand
What I want to eat,
She's given me this baby food
But all I want is a treat.

My mummy does not understand
What I want to drink,
She's given me some orange juice
But I need some time to think.

My mummy does not understand
What I want to do,
She smothers me all over
Would you like it if it was you?

My mummy does not understand
What I want to watch,
She's put on this weird girlie thing
But I want Elma doing hop scotch!

My mummy does not understand
What I'm trying to say,
She thinks I want to eat more food
But I want to go and play.

I wish I could have three wishes
And one of them would be
That I can actually talk to my mum
And to be let free.

Jade Heritage (11)
The Buckingham Secondary School, Buckingham

The CCTV Camera

I see you,
You don't see me.

Out in the street,
In the park,
By the cash box,
In the shop.

I see you,
You don't see me.

Eating your chips,
Having a jog,
Meeting your mates,
Playing a game.

I see you
You don't see me.

Feeling glum,
In a good mood,
Had a bad day,
Excited and happy.

I see you
You don't see me.

Looking around,
Scanning the area,
Peeking through gaps,
Hiding in fear.

I see you,
You don't see me.

Running away,
Twisting and turning,
Climbing high,
Tumbling low.

I see you,
You don't see me.

Marcus Prodanovic (12)
The Buckingham Secondary School, Buckingham

The Horrible Life Of A Tie

I get pulled up and down every day.
People chew on the tip of me.
I get flooded with saliva.
I get logos stamped on me, people throwing me on the floor.
I hang all day.
I get crumbs on me then brushed like a carpet.
I get thrown in the washing machine and go round and round.
I get left to dry to a crisp.
My life is boring because I'm a tie.

Ben Oxley (12)
The Buckingham Secondary School, Buckingham

The Feelings Inside

The loneliness inside is when you have no one to talk to.
The happiness inside is like a warm light inside us all.
The loneliness inside is where it's dark and cold.
Whereas in some it's always alight, but with others you may have
to look deeper inside.
There is loneliness inside when someone dies,
But you can't run from it because happiness will come to all some day,
But never fear it because loneliness will find all some day.

Katie Harland (11)
The Buckingham Secondary School, Buckingham

Feelings

Feelings are all around us
Feelings in you and me
Feelings are emotions
Emotions in you and me.

Emotions happen all around us
Emotions in you and me
Emotions show happiness or sadness
They're in you and me.

Happy, sad, excited, scared
Emotion in you and me
Brilliant, boring, cool, rubbish
Thoughts in you and me.

Thoughts are all around us
Thoughts about you and me
Thoughts can be bad and good
Thoughts in you and me.

Megan Thompson (12)
The Buckingham Secondary School, Buckingham

In Iraq

I sit and wait
I am reading the extract on death
I have been told to line up
The aircraft door opens
I run to my hiding place
My opposing team are waiting
The blood is rushing through my body
But butterflies are in my stomach
Sergeant calls for first shot
The first gunshots have fired
Bang! Bang!
Men are falling to the ground
Blood everywhere
My sergeant has fallen on the sandy bank
My men are down
I am the only one left
Wait a minute
A man over there
The other side are not down
I shoot my gun
I am too late.
He shoots his gun . . . I fall
My hands all bloody
I go pale
Blood pouring out of my mouth
He's won
I'm dead
I'm sorry.

Beth Cox (11)
The Buckingham Secondary School, Buckingham

Bags

I hate being a bag
You're always so sad
It's so annoying
I hate being a bag
You're always on somebody's back
It's so annoying
I hate being a bag
You always sit there
It's so annoying
I hate being a bag
You never get up
It's so annoying
I hate being a bag
You get stood on and you have to sit on the floor
It's *so* annoying!

Lee Morrison (12)
The Buckingham Secondary School, Buckingham

A Flower's Life

I sit here planted in the ground,
Lifeless with no heart to pound,
Miserable from night to day,
Motionless in the sunray.

Frantic people stomping about
Carrying a loud shout,
Careful not to stand on me,
I am not big like a tree.

I am sometimes a present,
Sitting, looking very pleasant,
I am placed in a lovely vase,
But prefer to be within the grass.

I sit here planted in the ground,
Lifeless with no heart to pound,
Miserable from night to day,
Motionless in the sunray.

Kirsty Grant (12)
The Buckingham Secondary School, Buckingham

Where Am I?

Someone was holding me,
Something felt soft upon my body,
I looked up, I looked down,
I looked left and right
There were colours, there were noises.

Where am I?

I felt someone lift me up and the cold air touched my body
I was being rocked, I was then shaken.

Where am I?

I was then laid down somewhere I did not like,
I tried to tell them but all that came out was . . .
Nothing!
I started crying, crying for someone to come get me,
I did not like it here!

Where am I?

Finally it had all gone dark,
None of the colours that I saw earlier today had appeared to me,
They had vanished, they were gone!
I knew I was safe because I was in someone's arms,
I knew where I was!

Kayley Roberts (12)
The Buckingham Secondary School, Buckingham

Woken Up Into The World

I was wrapped in a warm smooth blanket
I couldn't believe what I could hear,
People holding me, their voices loud and clear.
People crowding all around me,
Colours and big blobs that's what I could see.
At last I got moved to a colourful room,
I didn't know what was happening but I would soon.
The person carrying me said, 'This is your house you belong here,
                                                 it's your home.'
It was really weird; I wanted to be left alone.
A while later I was giggling loudly
After that I was having a picnic under the big oak tree.
The next thing I knew I was put into a uniform
Then put in the car and driven through a big cloudy storm.
Once I got out of the car my mum said,
'Be a good girl, it won't be long.'
I saw lots more kids just like me,
I think I knew where I was, at nursery!

Paige Costello (12)
The Buckingham Secondary School, Buckingham

Black

The world is spinning,
I am still,
Frozen in time,
I stand alone,
No sound, no movement.

Everything is dull,
No excitement,
Everyone looks like a cruel gargoyle,
No emotions.

Faces broken,
Souls are empty,
Full of distraught,
No colour,
No light.

The world is a dark, dull place,
No colour, no happiness in sight.
The sadness takes over.

Evan Wootton-Haley (11)
The Buckingham Secondary School, Buckingham

Blood

Why? Why?
The blood of our fathers,
The blood of our mothers,
The blood of our sisters,
The blood of our brothers,
The blood of our daughters,
Nannies and grans.
No good nor righteousness can cleanse your hands . . . of blood.
For you are evil, a bottomless hole
May the Lord cleanse your soul of sin, you are a servant of Satan
No honour, no feelings, no heart, lifeless corpses litter the street
For sin is a true art and you are a master.

Robert Lukey (11)
The Buckingham Secondary School, Buckingham

My Toys

What's your room like?
I know, mine's a tip,
Is yours?

When I leave my room
I always think my toys come alive,
Do you?

I feel sorry for mine,
Mum put them away all alone,
Do you?

My toys are always missing
Then they come back,
Do yours?

I hate putting them in the bin,
I sell them at a booty,
Do you?

Sam Reddrop (12)
The Buckingham Secondary School, Buckingham

I Will Be A . . .

I lay on my comfy bed,
I have thousands of thoughts running through my head,
I see the actors in my magazine, then I realise that will be me.
I will be a star,
I will be a star,
No matter what it takes, I'll make it far!
My idea is clear,
I will do what it takes,
I will be a star,
I will be the best, and I will make it there no matter what is said.

Hayley Siklodi (12)
The Buckingham Secondary School, Buckingham

What Do Sharks Do All Day?

Well . . .
At the bottom of the sea
On the ocean bed,
There lived a great white shark
And his little friend Fred.

So they get out of bed
To scratch their head
Then watch some telly
And fill with fish their hungry belly.

Every day at half-past three
They swim along the ocean to get their tea,
There was cod and mackerel, haddock and plaice
Yum! Lots of lovely fish to fill their face.

Then off they go
Back home again,
To splash and swim
In the pouring rain.

Abigail Young (12)
The Buckingham Secondary School, Buckingham

A Day In The Life Of An Abandoned Puppy

I'm standing, waiting, watching,
Hoping that someone will find me.
I'm all alone, left in the cold damp darkness.

Can anybody hear me?
I cry out with fear.
People walk, ignoring my cries, too busy to care.

What did I do to deserve this?
Why am I tied up in these strong, stinging strings?
I can't even move, my legs are so weak.
I lie down to rest forever.

Stephanie Robertson (11)
The Buckingham Secondary School, Buckingham

I Wish I Was Something Else

I've been sat on by fat and skinny bottoms
Boy, they sit on me for a long time!
I can't take it; I wish I was something else.
A bird flying in the sky, having freedom all to itself
No one sitting on it, I wish I was a bird.
I've been stood on by big and skinny legs
As hard as they can, how I wish I was something else.
A dog running around having no one stood on,
Having fresh air every day, I wish I was something else.
I wish I had a genie who listens to me
Makes my wishes come true, a real life too!

Geethapriya Thiruvalluvan (11)
The Buckingham Secondary School, Buckingham

Mum Why?

Mum why does the moon go up as the sun goes down?
Mum why is it hot in the summer and cold in the winter?
Mum why do girls have long hair and boys have short hair?
Mum?
Mum why do you never answer me?
Mum!

Charlotte Birks (12)
The Buckingham Secondary School, Buckingham

Football

Football, football,
Is the best, better than the rest.
Football, football,
Pass the ball; put the ball in the net.
Football, football,
Save the goal, kick the ball away from the goal.
Football, football,
We're going to lose.
Football, football,
We lost!
Football, football,
We're going to win, try our best to win.
Football, football,
There's the team, time to win, 1-0 up.
Football, football,
Best to win.
Football, football,
Half-time.
Football, football,
Next half.
We're going to win.
Football, football,
Yes, we won!
Football, football,
Hold the cup.

Kyle Carter (12)
The Buckingham Secondary School, Buckingham

Family

I love being with them

L aughing
O ver stupid things
V ery happy
E ven when

M oping
Y et we always find it

F unny
A nd they
M ake me
I ncredibly laugh and
L ove being there for
Y ou as I have found out in the past.

Cherry Eales (13)
The Buckingham Secondary School, Buckingham

A Day In The Life As A Chair

It starts at eight and ends at three
Children come and sit on me
Bags get put near my legs
And coats hung on my back.

Sometimes skinny bony people
Dig their bones into my plastic
When people draw on me,
It's silly the words like elastic.

Sometimes I get broken in two
And someone fixes me back
But always the wrong way round.
Maybe it's not that bad being a chair
But it's better when I'm not used or even when nobody's there.

Jasmine Harding (12)
The Buckingham Secondary School, Buckingham

The Horrible Day

I hate being a chair
You're always so lonely,
I hate being a chair
Even now it's very lonely.

I hate being a chair
You're always getting sat on,
I hate being a chair
They even stand on me.

I hate being a chair
I find it so boring
No one speaks to me
And I always get the end of everything.
Oh I hate being a chair
But it is just life.

Dale Armitage (11)
The Buckingham Secondary School, Buckingham

Stars

Stars at night
Seem so bright
Seem so little
At such a height
Shining through the glossy gloom
Look just like a little boom.

Wayde Cutler (11)
The Buckingham Secondary School, Buckingham

The Snowflake

For two days of last term we had snow.
A snowflake falls from the air, falls down and goes down your back.
The snowflake makes you want to shiver.
You walk out of the door and all you can see is white,
the white is pretty.
I love playing in the snow, throwing snowballs at people.
We have snowflakes, they are pretty.
We have snowflakes falling on your heads.
Snowflakes are white, they give you a shiver.

Amy Tickett (11)
The Buckingham Secondary School, Buckingham

Kittens

Little balls of fluff, so cute and so cuddly,
Chasing wool all night and day.
Purring at you and me and sleeping so peacefully,
Waking up in the morning time, yawning at the bright sunshine.

Alex Clinkard (11)
The Buckingham Secondary School, Buckingham

Nightmare

N ight is when I am asleep
I 'm a ghost in my dreams
G hosts go haunting in the night
H aunting is also what I do at night
T aste buds are waiting for me to activate
M onsters are under my bed
A wake the dead is what I do in my dreams
R esting in bed astonishingly in my dreams
E gypt is where I am in my dreams.

Jordan Klette (11)
The Buckingham Secondary School, Buckingham

Growing Up

When you're grown up
You could be a star,
You could be driving
In a big sports car.
You could be a singer
You could go quite far,
But then again you
Could be a footballer.
You could be a runner
In the Commonwealth Games
You could be a swimmer
Racing up and down the lanes.

Christina Jones (11)
The Buckingham Secondary School, Buckingham

Saying Goodbye

Saying goodbye to the one you love
You love him so much, you can't let him go
You just wait and he will come back to the one he loved.
You'll be together once again.
You cry lots of tears and the pain is so bad
You want him back, it makes you so sad.

Natasha Hedge (11)
The Buckingham Secondary School, Buckingham

The World War

It's night,
People are ready to fight.
In a far distance you can hear gunshots
You can hear pots smash,
Boom! You can hear people scream,
Snap! You can hear a stick breaking,
Crash!
Bash! You can hear a building crash.
Zap! You can almost hear a tank.
Bang! You can see a bank crash down.
Whoosh! You can hear the wind blowing.
The soldiers are going, Britain's won again.

Daniel Rolston (13)
The Buckingham Secondary School, Buckingham

War

Why is blood spilled in Iraq?
Why was the Second World War so harsh?
Why are there guns?
Why is there hatred in the world?
Why is there war?
When will it all stop?
When will there be peace?
When will the violence stop?
When will the shots halt?
When will the bombs drop?
What is the point of fighting?
What is the point of killing?
What is the point of violence?
What is the point of war?

Greg King (13)
The Buckingham Secondary School, Buckingham

My Poem

Why is the world full of war and hatred?
Why is there blood spilt on Iraq?
Why were so many lives taken when the Twin Towers
                                  got brought down?
Why do people want to kill others?
Why is there mass destruction in other countries?
What is the point in war?
Why do people get angry?
Why do I get angry?
Why is the world so violent?
Why do I feel violent?
What is the point!

James Blundell (12)
The Buckingham Secondary School, Buckingham

Fallen Family

Why does she love me?
Why does she hold me?
Why is she there when I need someone?
How does she know?
Why does she try always to make me smile?
Why does she shout sometimes?
Why is she even with my dad?
Why am I horrible to her?
What does she think of me now?
Why does she try to get rid of me half the time?
Why does she say she loves me, 'cause I don't wanna know.
Why does she always run up to me and hug me?
Why though, why?
Why does she want a dog instead of me?
Why does she act sweet to me in front of my dad?
Why is she destroying my dad?
Why does she care for me?
Why have I got a bit inside that tells me to love her?
Why does she look out for me when I have my dad?
I know, she just wants to be a mother to me.
Why does my dad not listen to me?
Why is he trying to get me to like her?
Why does she have to come everywhere with us?

Zoe McPartlane (13)
The Buckingham Secondary School, Buckingham

For The Speed

Maybe they can go fast or perhaps they go slow
Dark or light they come in all colours
Illegally and frantically they chase other versions,
You can identify them, even in the dark as they light up dangerously
They roar or purr like a cat being stroked
Adventurously boom down the high street
Rapidly jumping into a space
Suddenly they stop and it's all quiet.

Conor Yull (13)
The Buckingham Secondary School, Buckingham

The Poem Of Life

Life is a funny thing, sometimes good, sometimes bad.
You can't avoid it, it's yours for good.
You may love it, you may hate it but you can't escape it.
You may want to take it away; someone else may want to take it away.
It's made for you, no one else, young or old, they're all the same
It's what you do with it that counts.

Jack Carroll-Taylor (12)
The Buckingham Secondary School, Buckingham

A Friend Is Like A Special Gift

A friend is like a special gift,
You have to look after them and they look after you.
They can sometimes break up with you
But in the end the pieces are all put back together again.
A friend in need is a friend indeed.
You have to gain their trust and they gain yours
Because a friend is like a special gift
If it breaks, the pieces are all put together again,
And if a friend breaks up with you
The pieces are all put back together again.

Jordan Stephens (12)
The Buckingham Secondary School, Buckingham

Sorry

I'm sorry for what I told you
And also 'cause it's true,
But I can't help,
The way I feel 'bout you.

I feel so stupid
So little and all wrong,
My life now feels so empty
Like a slow, sad song.

Every time you walk away
A tear falls down my face,
And now when you see me
You pick up the pace.

I'm sorry for what I told you
And also 'cause it's true,
But I can't help
The way I feel 'bout you.

Jade Muckleston (12)
The Buckingham Secondary School, Buckingham

I Wonder

I wonder if Grandad's looking down on me
I wonder if he watches me.
I wonder if he is proud of me.
I wonder if he would've liked to meet me.
I wonder if he will be in my heart.
I wonder if he's watching me now.
I wonder if he sees me in Heaven.
I wonder if he knows who I am.
I wonder if he talks to me.
I wonder if I'll ever see him.
I wonder if he loves me
I wonder if he is with me.

Kelly Allen (13)
The Buckingham Secondary School, Buckingham

The Pencil

We all squash in together, both pen and pencil
As she picks us up and chucks us on the windowsill.
I squeal and yelp and shout and scream for help
But no one can hear me.
They don't know we really exist,
Except from when we are in their hand.
Writing till all that's left of lead is only a strand.
We scream and shout and we wiggle about
But no one can see us.
I'm nothing but a pencil, small not tall,
I'm nothing but a pencil, nothing at all.

Sharn Duggan (13)
The Buckingham Secondary School, Buckingham

A Day In The Life Of A Turtle

I'm a turtle, a turtle.
I ride the waves all over the world.
I'm a turtle, a turtle.
I cruise the Caribbean looking for a mate.
I'm a turtle, a turtle.
I surf the Australian current.
I'm a turtle, a turtle.
I patrol round the multicoloured reef.
I'm a turtle, a turtle I am.

Josh Whitehead (13)
The Buckingham Secondary School, Buckingham

Success

When you try so hard you will finally succeed.
Whether the first time the ball reaches a net
Or the discus throws further than you can imagine,
Your experience will keep you smiling.
Your confidence will start low but practice will soon solve the problem,
Just try your best and soon faith will take care of the rest.

Stevie Watts (13)
The Buckingham Secondary School, Buckingham

Size Zero Models

I wonder why they look like that,
I wonder why they feel fat,
Being size zero isn't cool,
Starving yourself doesn't rule!
Being as thin as a stick
Doesn't make you look that fit.
Being curvy is the best,
Loving food and the rest,
Being sick every night
Doesn't make you at all that bright!

Kelly-Ann Morris (13)
The Buckingham Secondary School, Buckingham

A Life As A Planner

It always starts at eight in the morning
Screaming and shouting is all I hear
I have a timetable in the back
Homework in the middle with instructions on the front
And if you get stuck I have information near the back.
When the lesson begins I get thrown around all over
It all quietens down but I still end up on the ground.
I stay in a bag all lunch; it's all very noisy outside
But the only time I get to go outside is when I have to sit with Year 9.

Maddie Smith (13)
The Buckingham Secondary School, Buckingham

The Beach

The beach is calm
My toes in the sand
The cool breeze blowing
Through the crowds of people

The birds swoop down low
And peak at the fish
People go to the well
And make a wish

The ice cream van comes
Faces light up
They get their ices
Yummy yup!

Stephanie Lambourne (13)
The Buckingham Secondary School, Buckingham

A Day On The Street

I saw two ladies today
Dressed nicely, food, money.
I have none of that.

I saw a family today,
Happy, smiling, loving.
I'm not happy, I'm not smiling, I'm not loved.
I have none of that.

I saw some children today,
Having fun, eating sweets, chatting.
I'm not fun and I have no sweets, I have no one to chat to.
I have none of that.

I saw two men in a pub today,
Drinking, eating, smiling.
I can't drink, I have no money to eat, I have no reason to smile.
I have none of that.

The reason I have none of that,
Happiness, family, money,
It's because I'm . . . I'm . . .
Homeless.

Samantha Horsler (13)
The Buckingham Secondary School, Buckingham

Lost Heart

I seem to have a problem
I think I've lost my heart
I can't find it anywhere
It's like I'm searching through the dark.

For a second it was like I wasn't there
I couldn't hear anything or feel anything
It was as if I was in despair
I was finding it hard to breathe
I was desperate to leave then
I was getting rattled
I didn't know what to do
Then I suddenly remembered
My heart belongs to you.

Sean Elmes (13)
The Buckingham Secondary School, Buckingham

Life As A Table

It all starts at 8am, the noisy lot come in.
Every day they come in shouting and screaming,
Things on me get flung on the floor.

The bags get banged on top of me.
It hurts so much, so much pain.
They have no idea that those bags are heavy,
I think I'll break!

Lesson has started the writing tickles so bad,
Turning pages and even writing on me,
They write and put even more stuff on me.

Lunch is here, no time for a rest,
They keep dropping their food on me.
Oh what's that? A drop of juice!
Maybe it's not that bad.

Home time at last, the school is so quiet,
Now may I can get my rest
But then again they will be back in the morning
Now for sleep, night-night.

Becky Davies (12)
The Buckingham Secondary School, Buckingham

Bad Hair Day
(Inspired by Vicky Pollard - Little Britain)

No but yer but no but yer!
I'm 'avin' such a bad day with me 'air
Yer but no but yer but no!
This flippin' top knot just won' go!

So I got up really early this mornin'
Like about half-past eight,
Meetin' me mates down the park la'er,
So I really can't be late.

I put me favourite tracksuit on,
Me brigh' pink chavvy one,
Time to do me 'air now,
Great start, me brush 'as gone!

Finally found me 'airbrush but
Me top knot won't go right,
It won't go 'igh enough on me 'ead,
Oh my god, I look such a sight!

Maybe I'll try it more on the side,
No, that don't suit me at all,
Oops, I've broken me 'airbrush again,
I lobbed it at me wall.

I think it's finally takin' shape,
It's finally goin' right,
Time to put me 'airbobble in,
Come on, I'm up for a fight!

Just got back from the park now,
I've got a new boyfriend or two,
'Ad a busy day natterin' on
The whole thing starts again tomorrow!

No but yer but no but yer,
I've 'ad such a bad day with me 'air
Yer but no but yer but no
My chavvy top knot's perfect now!

Sophie Ellis (13)
The Warriner School, Banbury

Model Behaviour

There's a tall girl with a tiny waist
She's got prominent cheekbones and a pretty face,
Giving her all for the camera,
Then she's airbrushed to perfect her.

Kate Moss is strutting the new Burberry line,
Bare-faced but more than fine,
Her flawless look makes girls stare,
They think, *she's so lucky, it's not fair!*

Every girl has dreamed to be thin,
With a flat stomach so she resembles a pin.
Slimming pills can help teenage weight loss
They hope to look like Lily Cole or Kate Moss.

To help them fit into their size zero skinny jeans,
Models take laxatives, eat water and goji beans,
But in real life model diets aren't practical
And things they eat aren't even edible!

I pity these girls because they can't eat real food
And then walk the catwalks almost in the nude,
So ditch the diet have fries and burger
'Cause we want models who are a lot curvier!

Cara Davis (12)
The Warriner School, Banbury

Stop With The Homework

Please stop, please stop,
Don't give me anymore.
I'm fed up with all this homework
Or I will walk out the door!

Please stop, please stop,
This homework I don't like,
This maths is making me tired
Or I will go on strike.

Please stop, please stop,
This homework is making me dizzy.
I really can't cope anymore
I am already busy.

Please stop, please stop
I've already got lots to do.
This science is taking over me,
Down with the thumbs, *boohoo!*

Please stop, please stop,
I really don't like what I see.
This art is really boring
Please just leave me be!

Please stop, please stop,
This homework is not exciting.
Give me something fun
And I will start writing.

Sian Murphy (13)
The Warriner School, Banbury

Tea And Scones

One's great county has many sports
The key to our progress has been our courts.
To hold the Olympics, progress is fast
Wembley stadium in concrete is cast.

Government taxes are forever more
Unfortunately none is given to the poor.
Fossil fuels are powering us skyward
Renewable energy is the only way forward.

The number of obese children is very disturbing
Deaths by obesity just keeps rising.
The number of closed hospitals is very surprising
The NHS just keeps depriving.

Al the paedophiles just keep escaping
Nobody stops them, they just keep raping.
So this is the end of one's moaning
Now everyone go back to one's tea and sconing.

James Richardson (12)
The Warriner School, Banbury

Big Brother

It was first about a cube
And then about a chicken,
It was a silly argument
But it nearly went to kicking.

It was just Shilpa and Jade
But then Danielle joined in,
She said, 'Go off back home'
And Big Brother called her in!

Big Bro asked why she said that
She answered, 'I don't remember'
I think she was lying
Whilst Jade couldn't keep her temper.

Despite all of this happening
There was one clear winner,
Shilpa came in first
After undercooking the dinner!

George Kay (12)
The Warriner School, Banbury

Disabled Children

I'm sitting here writing this poem
Even though I don't now how
And I can't even spell
I've tried many things now
But none of them work.

How am I meant to do this?
I'm disabled I can't do a thing.
I'm not pretty, I'm not fun, I'm not clever,
I'm just the girl that you all hate!

Crying here alone now
All these things that keep going wrong
I can't believe I have to read this out
I will just make a fool of myself.

All those people staring at me as if I am not real
What have I done?
I'm just one of you!
But nobody cares
I'm just that thick girl sat in the corner!

I wish I was like the normal people!
They are clever, they are pretty, they are normal!
So why aren't I the same?
How do I cope?
I'm so different to all of them.

All you people you don't think of me or how I feel,
It's hard for me, no friends, no one to play with.
If you had a heart you would talk to me and see how I feel,
I'm all alone, alone and afraid.

Megan Collison (13)
The Warriner School, Banbury

Young Writers Information

We hope you have enjoyed reading this book - and that you will continue to enjoy it in the coming years.

If you like reading and writing poetry drop us a line, or give us a call, and we'll send you a free information pack.

Alternatively if you would like to order further copies of this book or any of our other titles, then please give us a call or log onto our website at www.youngwriters.co.uk

**Young Writers Information
Remus House
Coltsfoot Drive
Peterborough
PE2 9JX**

(01733) 890066